Fly for their Lives

Dedication
To all the rescue helicopter winchmen and aircrewmen, especially to the late Master Air Loadmasters David Bullock and Peter Barwell.

Fly for their Lives

John Chartres

Airlife
England

Copyright © John Chartres 1988

First published 1988
by Airlife Publishing Ltd.

Chartres, John
    Fly for their lives.
    1. Search and rescue operations—Great
    Britain—History
    I. Title
    363.3'48   TL553.8

    ISBN 0-906393-93-0

Printed in England by Livesey Ltd., Shrewsbury.

Airlife Publishing Ltd.

7 St. John's Hill, Shrewsbury, England.

Contents

Acknowledgements

My special thanks go again to the Air Historical Branch (RAF) and especially to its Director, Air Commodore Henry Probert, RAF (Retd); to Group Captain T. C. Flanagan, MSc, BA (Hons), RAF (Retd) and to Mr Sebastian Cox, the last for his help in the compilation of the 'Famine Relief' chapter.

They also go to the many readers of the Royal Air Forces Association journal *Air Mail* who responded to my appeals for help in its obviously well-read columns. Some, but not all, are mentioned by name in the text and picture captions but it is they who have 'brought life' to official accounts by their personal reminiscences and generous loans of photographs. As a professional journalist I remain deeply impressed by the 'pulling power' of this publication and wish to thank its Editor for publishing my letters.

I would like to thank many serving members of all three Services, especially the friends I feel proud to keep in the helicopter rescue units of both the RAF and the FAA. Similar thanks go to other friends in what was British Airways Helicopters; in the Bristow organisation and in the relatively new Bond Helicopters Ltd. I made new and valued friends within the RAF Transport Force at Lyneham during research into the Famine Relief chapter.

Again I have had much help from the Fleet Air Arm Museum at Yeovilton and from the Museum of Army Flying at Middle Wallop.

Two old friends in the rather close world of aviation history have again come to *my* rescue with essential facts and pictures — James D. Ferguson of Aberdeen and Brian Robinson of Stockport.

Finally I would like to thank Ian Allan Ltd, publishers of my earlier books, *Helicopter Rescue, Sea King, Shackleton* and *Nimrod* for permission to use material which I gleaned during research into those publications. I have also used, when possible with the permission of authors and publishers, the following books as references:

Maritime is Number Ten, written and published by Kevin Baff, South Australia.
Boat in the Blue, by W. D. Pereira (Line One Publishing Ltd).
The Supermarine Walrus, by Lieutenant Commander G. W. R. Nicholl (G. T. Foulis and Co Ltd).
Royal Air Force 1939-45, by Denis Richards and Hilary St G. Saunders (HMSO).
Down in the Drink, by Ralph Barker (Pan Books).
The Last Enemy, by Richard Hillary (Pan Books).
The Sea Shall Not Have Them, by John Harris (Hurst & Blackett Ltd).
Monograph on Air Sea Rescue, author anonymous (HMSO).

Terminology

I have endeavoured to use the terminology appropriate to the periods in which incidents occurred, thus some airspeeds will be given in mph, others in knots, etc. I have avoided too much 'metrication' as indeed does most of the aviation world, so that distances will be given in statute or nautical miles and heights in feet.

There will be references to 'wireless sets' and 'wireless operators' up to the middle 1950s when NATO standardised the word 'radio'. (Just to confuse, of course, even in World War 2 morse communications were 'wireless telegraphy' and speech communications were 'radio telephony'.)

Author's Preface

The idea for the compilation of this book partly arose out of a discussion with some close friends who sincerely believe that world peace can only be achieved through the total abolition of all armed forces. While not attempting to destroy their fundamental argument I ventured to point out that the Royal Air Force alone has saved many, many, more lives than it has 'taken' since the end of the Second World War. They were a little surprised.

The argument can be advanced that non-combatants, even doctors and nurses, are belligerents in that they, like tank recovery crews, are assisting 'instruments of war' to fight another day. That is an argument which could go on to the end of time and might have been applicable to the wartime Air-Sea-Rescue services. Since the 1950s, however, a new dimension has emerged in that aircraft of all three UK Armed Forces rescue about ten times as many civilians as the fellow-Servicemen they are strictly provided to assist.

Certainly it is accepted that war, and the preparation for it, with accompanying urgency and relative absence of financial restraint, accelerates many advances in medicine surgery and other fields for the ultimate benefit of mankind. That factor has certainly applied in the field of 'Search and Rescue' by aircraft in this and many other nations.

Details and pictures of a number of incidents related in this book have been published before, some in my own books, but I have endeavoured to put between the covers of one volume a comprehensive story of the development of this very special form of aviation. I do not claim it to be a 'history'. With United Kingdom air rescues alone running at the rate of about 1,000 a year and the grand total of *civilians* in distress aided approaching the 50,000 mark, such a work would have to run into many volumes and would be of limited interest anyway.

I hope this book will please and give pride to, those who have been and still are, involved in this special art; and that it will interest and be read by many others at a time when this form of 'service' is apt to be taken for granted by the general public.

J. C.
Hale, Cheshire, January 1987.

Foreword

By Admiral of the Fleet Lord Lewin, K.G., G.C.B., L.V.O., D.S.C.

For as long as man has ventured on the surface of the sea the sailor has known it to be his implacable enemy. Sometimes smiling, sometimes angry, always deceptive, never to be trusted, for thousands of years the sailor knew that if he were cast adrift his chances of rescue or survival were small, yet in a generation that situation has changed dramatically. We accept that we travelled the world before the aeroplane and that now we travel more quickly, we know that warfare was deadly before the aeroplane and that now it is more deadly still, but we do not appreciate so well the difference the aeroplane has made to the task of searching for the shipwrecked mariner and saving life at sea. This book tells the history of search and rescue by aircraft from the very beginning to the present day, and an inspiring story it is. As so often in technical development, war provided the opportunity and the necessity for experiment in both search and rescue techniques. While it is easily recognised that the speed of aircraft widens the area that can be searched in a given time, the agonising difficulty of spotting a survivor in a tiny dinghy in a rough sea needs to be experienced: this led to the production of aids to identification, first visual, then electronic. Experience again showed how difficult it is, having found the survivor, often exhausted and unable to help himself, to pluck him to safety in anything but the calmest sea. Sadly in the war such experience was all too easy to come by, but unlike much that war teaches us the lessons learned have been put to invaluable use in peace. The sea remains as dangerous as ever, and the explosion in the numbers taking to the sea in small boats round our coasts is always increasing the numbers at risk. We now take the provision of the Search and Rescue Services for granted, it is salutary to be reminded of the price paid to reach the present pitch of efficiency.

John Chartres, whose research must have been extensive, has comprehensively covered the development of search and rescue from the beginnings to the present day and has illustrated his record with many dramatic first hand accounts. After a lifetime in the Royal Navy, and now as President of The Shipwrecked Mariners Society, which makes two awards for outstanding rescues each year, I have never ceased to be amazed at the courage and skill displayed by those in the Search and Rescue Services. Almost by definition, if a rescue is required — the weather is bad. It requires a special sort of calm calculated bravery, not of the sort engendered in action against an enemy, to tackle the situations that these men often face, and the decisions of life and death must be made by the men on the spot. We are lucky to have such men and can be very proud of them.

Chapter One
Introduction

In a corner of the Royal Air Force Museum at Hendon there stands the body of a heroic pigeon — that of His Majesty's Pigeon Number NURP/17/F/16331 no less — and in a corner of the Fleet Air Arm Museum at Yeovilton there can be found a message form bearing the handwritten words: 'H-12 N8666. We have landed to pick up DH4 crew about 50E by N of Yarmouth. Sea too rough to get off. Will you please send for us as soon as

His Majesty's Pigeon Number NURP/17/F/16331 as preserved by officers of the Royal Naval Air Station, Great Yarmouth, in 1917 and displayed by them under a plaque describing him as a 'Very Gallant Gentleman'. He is still to be seen in the Royal Air Force Museum at Hendon as one who played a gallant part in the first recorded 'air-sea rescue'.

possible as boat is leaking. We are taxi-ing W. by S. V. Nicholl.'

These two exhibits commemorate the first fully recorded air-sea rescue operation in aviation history. It took place in September 1917. Its story has been recorded before, first in the book *The Story of a North Sea Air Station* by C. F. Snowden Gamble, and in my own book *Helicopter Rescue*, but it deserves repetition here because it demonstrates many basic principles and problems which have affected the whole art of the saving of life by aircraft and from aircraft up to the present day.

The saga began when a Curtiss H-12 Large America flying boat and a de Havilland 4 landplane of the Royal Naval Air Service engaged Zeppelin *L44* in combat near Terschelling Island off the east coast of the North Sea. The British aircraft shot the Zeppelin down between them but return fire damaged the DH4's radiator and its pilot, Flight Lieutenant A. H. H. Gilligan, RNAS, had to ditch.

He and his Observer, Flight Lieutenant G. H. Trewin, were unhurt and the pilot of the flying boat, Squadron Commander Vincent Nicholl, alighted alongside, with his port engine running rough on one bank of cylinders and one magneto. In the landing (or 'alighting' to use the more appropriate term) the starboard wingtip float was carried away and the hull strained. The DH4 crew were, however, able to swim across from their sinking aircraft and climb into the by now badly leaking H-12, making 'six souls on board', the others being the second pilot, Flight Lieutenant R. Reckie; the wireless operator, Air Mechanic Thompson and the engineer, A. M. Walk.

With no possibility of taking off from a roughish sea with a missing wingtip float,

1

A Curtiss H-12 'Large America' flying boat of the type used during the encounter with the Zeppelin in September 1917.

Commander Nicholl set about a long sea-taxi towards the English coast and his home base at Great Yarmouth. His best course would have been 260 degrees but on that bearing seas were threatening to pull the bows under so he settled for 300 degrees which, while taking him a long way north, kept him headed into wind and wave. Commander Nicholl arranged watch systems under which five men baled continuously while a sixth had a two-hour 'rest' clinging to the outer struts of the port wing to keep the float-less starboard one out of the sea.

The H-12 carried, like all the RNAS boats, four pigeons, and they were despatched in pairs at an interval of 48 hours. The first pair each carried the message referred to above; the second pair one reading: '3 pm. Very urgent. Seaplane 8666 to CO Air Station Great Yarmouth. We have sighted nothing. The wind has been drifting us WNW ever since we landed so we may have missed Cromer. We are not far from the coast as we keep seeing small land birds. Sea is still rough. Machine still intact. We will fire Very lights every five minutes tonight. V. Nicholl.'

One of the second pair of pigeons reached Great Yarmouth on 7 September. That day too a young Army officer walking his girl friend on a beach near the air station picked up the body of 'F/16331' lying on the sand, apparently having died from exhaustion. The officer (Second Lieutenant D. W. Hughes of the Monmouthshires) spotted the message clip and abandoning anything else he intended to do that evening contacted the air base. The two messages were then interpreted

and circulated to the various rescue agencies which had been searching for the overdue airmen for three days but which had just stood down.

A very skilled navigator, Lieutenant Commander B. S. Bannerman, RN, Captain of the gunboat HMS *Halcyon,* based at Lowestoft, worked out the probable drift of the flying boat from its first recorded position to its second estimated one under the prevailing wind, tide and sea conditions and set off; with a tiny Schneider seaplane perched on the aft deck for a possible final close air search. In fact Commander Bannerman found HM Flying Boat *8666* just about where he had calculated it would be — about 100 miles north-east of Great Yarmouth.

All aboard were alive but certainly not well. They had been aboard the leaking flying boat for four days and four nights. The engine fuel had soon run out and they had had to resort to drifting with a drogue sea-anchor holding them into wind and wave. They had been reduced to drinking rusty water from the engine radiators and all were suffering from exhaustion and sea-sickness although the baling-out of the leaking hull had to be maintained continuously. Flight Lieutenant Leckie was suffering from internal bleeding when rescued but was still wielding a baling can.

In the event not only were all six rescued but HM Flying Boat *8666* was towed in to Great Yarmouth to be repaired and to fly again in the often unsung war against U-boats in the North Sea in the First World War. The officers of the RNAS station at Great

Yarmouth had the body of Pigeon F/16331 stuffed and mounted on a silver plinth bearing the words: 'A Very Gallant Gentleman' and kept it in their Mess. Happily, and for posterity, his little body remains on view at Hendon.

Many of the circumstances of that operation were to be repeated in World War 2 and many of the lessons it taught hold good even in the present helicopter and maritime reconnaissance aircraft age of life-saving with all the sophisticated search and survival equipment evolved over seventy years. Perhaps the most important lesson learned was the necessity of the will to survive by the victims of an accident. The importance of communications to base was, of course, dramatically illustrated. Pigeons did remain in service well into World War 2 as later chapters will record.

The importance of combinations of good airmanship and good *seamanship* by both survivors and rescuers was amply demonstrated, particularly by Commander Bannerman's navigational skills. (In recent years it has been suggested that navigators could be regarded as redundant in rescue helicopters because of modern press-button kit but there has been many an instance when a skilled 'Nav' has worked out just where a drifting inflatable dinghy with two frightened children aboard could be found at first light the morning after the alarm was raised.)

The incident also demonstrated the limitation of the flying boat when it comes to

The survivors being brought home.

alighting on, and taking off from, the open sea. A later chapter will record how often Commander Nicholl's experience of losing a wingtip float or sustaining hull damage was to be repeated, sometimes with far more disastrous consequences; even with much more sophisticated aircraft than his H-12 — including the apparently indestructible Sunderlands and Catalinas of World War 2.

In the immediate post-First World War years the lessons learned from the rescue of the H-12 and DH4 crews were retained, like many others, by far-sighted officers of both the Royal Navy and the recently created Royal Air Force. Like so many other lessons from the First World War however, they tended to be ignored by politicians and others in high places (mainly bent on protecting taxpayers' money and thereby earning popularity) so that the development of air-sea rescue techniques only moved forward very slowly until just after the outbreak of World War 2 when some very sharp lessons indeed were taught.

Fortunately for the lives of many thousands of Servicemen and civilians an important component of the small between-the-wars Royal Air Force was created and called 'Coastal Area Command' consisting in the main of the former Royal Naval Air Service flying boat squadrons. Using the former RNAS squadron numbers and adding the digits '20' to them they called themselves the 'Flying Boat Union' and in one of those touches which distinguish the British armed forces from all others they refused to polish their buttons so that they took on a 'sea green hue'.

The valiant Curtiss H-12s, the 'Porte Babies' and the 'Felixstowe Furies' were replaced by Supermarine Southamptons and then after only a few years by such biplane flying boats as the Blackburn Iris and Perth, the Short Rangoon and Singapore and the Saro London.

The 'Flying Boat Union' squadrons took their aircraft all over the vast-flung British Empire and to other parts of the world, making the nation's presence felt and proving that long-range aeroplanes could carry out tasks undreamed of before the outbreak of World War 1.

In the context of this book it very quickly

became clear that flying boats needed efficient *non*-flying boats to attend to their needs and to ensure their efficiency and safety. Thus was born what was later to be styled the RAF Marine Branch, an organisation which combined aviation and nautical skills and which laid the foundations of the first structure of an air-sea rescue service. The first 'RAF boats' were modest little vessels, really just minor improvements on the RNAS craft which had tended the H-12s and others at such bases as Great Yarmouth and Felixstowe, helping launch them, bring them ashore and occasionally picking up aircrew when things went amiss. There were about 200 of them, called pinnaces or tenders, capable of anything between five and fifteen knots. On the flying boat stations one was always designated as the 'Safety' or 'Crash' boat.

In the late 1920s and early 1930s flying boats and seaplanes (and the distinction must always be made — flying boats having wings and boat-shaped hulls, seaplanes being ordinary aeroplanes with floats instead of wheels as their undercarriages) became much faster. Not only did airspeeds increase but so did take-off and 'alighting' speeds. During a number of the Schneider Trophy contests the RAF had to borrow fast coastal motor boats from the Royal Navy to cater for safety and rescue requirements.

Much faster flying boats in the monoplane configuration were on the drawing boards in the 1930s, one particular design culminating in the Imperial Airways 'C-Class', later to be modified into the immortal Sunderland, and safety requirements for take-off and alighting speeds of some 75 knots had to be considered.

As so often happens the 'men of the hour' were available. They included Mr Hubert Scott-Paine, a noted water speed record breaker and head of a firm called the British Power Boat Company, and an Aircraftman Shaw, RAF, earlier known as Colonel T. E. Lawrence, who was spending one of his reclusion periods at RAF Mount Batten while trying to withdraw from fame as 'Lawrence of Arabia'.

Hubert Scott-Paine drew a set of designs for hard-chined launches, capable of attaining thirty-plus knots within seconds of their leaving moorings. His concept was that

they should be between 40 and 50 ft long, would have a draught of less than three feet at anchor and would 'plane-up' at speed reducing the effective draught to less than two feet. (This 'planing' ability, which every modern dinghy sailor or speedboat enthusiast understands, was to produce not only very high speeds with only about a third of the hull length absorbing friction from the water but also to enable RAF rescue launches to skim through minefields.)

In 1932 the first of a batch of '200-Class Seaplane Tenders' was delivered to the RAF with its sea trials conducted by AC1 Shaw. The boat, built by the British Power Boat Company at Hythe, Southampton, was 37 feet 6 in long and its two Power Meadows engines gave it a top speed of 27 knots. Four years later (in a curious transposition of numbers) the first of '100-Class' High Speed Launches was delivered to RAF Calshot. It had three Napier Lion engines each developing 500 hp and could reach forty

A 50-ft Motor Torpedo Boat built in World War 1 and used by the RAF for high speed flight rescue duties between 1927 and 1933. Powered by three Thornycroft 350 hp engines. Maximum speed 45 knots.

A 63-ft High Speed Launch built in 1941-42 by the British Power Boat Company *(RAF)*.

knots with an operating range of 500 miles. It provided the foundation for the RAF's High Speed Launch fleet which was to play such a significant, if belated, part in the rescue of downed airmen throughout World War 2.

In the years immediately after World War 1 very little special equipment or organisation was provided for airmen who might have to ditch into, or parachute, into the sea. In the 'piping days of peace' most RAF landplanes only flew over land. Nevertheless aircraft of 'The Fleet Air Arm of the Royal Air Force' — that is landplanes and seaplanes operating from aircraft carriers — obviously did fly over the sea most of the time.

For many years the rescue of airmen flying from aircraft carriers and getting into trouble was entrusted to attendant destroyers which always steamed alongside such carriers as HMS *Courageous*. Fleet Air Arm aeroplanes were, however, provided with flotation bags, stowed perhaps somewhere in the tail or amidships where there was nothing else of importance to get in the way. The only RAF aircrew provided with any sort of rescue equipment were those in the flying boats who were provided with inflatable triangular dinghies from 1925 onwards.

In 1935 Fleet Air Arm aircraft were supplied with 'Youngman' dinghies in three sizes and fitted to the upper wings of biplanes so that with good luck an expensive aeroplane such as a Fairey Seal might stay afloat as well as its crew, all to be recovered and thus saving the taxpayer a lot of money.

The first Royal Air Force High Speed Launch, No 100, was handed over at Manston, Kent, in August 1936. It was a significant location because the RAF station there was to remain one of the most important life-saving bases in the United Kingdom up to the present day where it houses 'E' Flight of No 22 Helicopter Rescue Squadron with responsibility for the lives of many, many people who can get into trouble in the 'corner' of the English Channel and the North Sea. (Apart from its importance in the Battle of Britain and as a fighter station throughout World War 2 Manston earned a place in history as the aerodrome from where the first foul weather helicopter rescue in this country was launched and as one of the last bases where a foam carpet could be laid for emergency landings.)

It has sometimes been argued that politicians and senior officers of the RAF in the 1930s did not properly visualise that the most important air battles in the world's history would be fought first over the Channel and then over the North Sea and the Atlantic and that insufficient preparations were made for an air-sea rescue service. It has been wisely said, however, that hindsight is a very fine thing, and in any case those with foresight had to battle for a slice of a very small defence budget cake.

In 1936 and 1937 the Air Staff considered the fitting of flotation gear to landplanes and it was decided that Fleet Air Arm aircraft, General Reconnaissance and Torpedo Bomber types as well as flying boats should be equipped with emergency dinghies, marine distress signals and positive buoyancy. In May 1938 it was agreed that the 'heavy' bombers of the time — Harrows, Whitleys, Heyfords and Hampdens — should carry

Lysander/Launch co-operation. The launch is HSL *116* built by the British Power Boat Company with three Napier Sea Lion engines. Rescue gear can be seen mounted on the Lysander spat stub wings *(RAF)*.

multi-seat 'H' type circular dinghies. Medium bombers such as Battles and Blenheims were to be equipped with 'C' type triangular dinghies. A large 'J' type dinghy capable of accommodating seven or eight survivors was developed at this time for the next generation of four-engined heavies.

With the war clouds looming close in the winter of 1938-39 it became possible to base seven High Speed Launches around the coastline at Manston, Felixstowe, Donibristle, Calshot (two boats) and Pembroke Dock. The deployment of this tiny fleet left, however, some four hundred miles of the North Sea coast uncovered and the AOC in C of Bomber Command (then Air Chief Marshal Sir E. R. Ludlow Hewitt) needed to exercise his aircraft over just this sea area. Even though most of his main Striking Force aircraft had by then been fitted with dinghies the crews chances of survival from a ditching would have been slender, especially in the winter months.

At a conference in February 1939 it was decided that the rescue launch organisation should be placed under the control of Coastal Command and that an extra thirteen launches should be ordered, to include two for Middle East Command. Since they would take nearly a year to build, two boats allocated to the Far East were diverted to Grimsby and Great Yarmouth and the Donibristle launch was moved south to Blyth thus giving improved cover of the North Sea.

During Home Defence exercises in August 1938 and 1939 Coastguards were asked to keep a special watch for distress signals from aircraft marking the beginning of this Service's involvement with air-sea rescue which has been maintained to the present day. The Navy's involvement was also marked by the provision of a number of destroyers with rescue responsibilities.

Between the wars, therefore, foundations, albeit slender ones, *were* laid for a service which would have to expand rapidly even though it came under the 'too little and too late' category in the opening phases of the conflict. At that stage the structure of the service only envisaged the saving of airmen's lives by surface craft. The use of aircraft *to* save lives beyond the search phase was to come much later.

In June 1940, just before the main onslaught, there were still only fourteen High Speed Launches in commission at the original bases plus Kirkwall (Orkney), Lerwick (Shetland), Aberdeen and Guernsey. The responsibility for searching for downed aircraft and aircrew remained with their 'owners', their own squadrons which were expected to use their own operational aircraft.

History has shown that the really critical factor for both sides in the Battle of Britain was the availability of pilots. Of the 220 aircrew killed or reported missing in the last three weeks of July 1940 the vast majority had disappeared over the sea. Although no precise statistics were available it was assessed that a great many fighter pilots may have baled out or ditched successfully only to die of exposure within sight of shore. This tragic waste, which so nearly lost the battle for the British, led to an early and hasty *ad hoc* arrangement between Air Vice-Marshal Keith Park (AOC 11 Group) and Vice-Admiral Sir Bertram H. Ramsay (Vice-Admiral, Dover) to bring in light naval craft to supplement the handful of RAF launches, and to draw on some Lysander Army Co-operation aircraft (which had proved unsatisfactory in their designated role) to act as spotters thus providing the basis for an inter-service organisation and one which recognised the need for specialist search aircraft.

It had been noted at an early stage of the Battle of Britain that the Luftwaffe, as a part of all its other preparations for war, had a far superior rescue service established in peacetime, employing Heinkel 59 seaplanes, sometimes backed up by launches, together with permanently moored 'Sea Rescue Floats', code-named 'Lobster Pots' by the RAF. The Heinkels carried collapsible boats, medical stores and radio; and the Floats, placed about half-way across the Channel, were fitted out with bunks, dry clothing, food and water. (The Floats were later copied and 21 British versions, including some German ones which had drifted ashore and had been improved, were moored in the Channel and the North Sea. These were code-named 'Cuckoos' but there is only one record of successful use.)

Perhaps most importantly the pilots of the Luftwaffe's single-seat fighters had one-man

A Heinkel He 59 rescue seaplane displaying the Red Cross symbol *(Bruce Robertson collection).*

dinghies, bags of fluorescine marker dye and other survival aids whereas RAF fighter pilots were totally dependent on their Mae West life jackets. Luftwaffe bombers had emergency wireless transmitters which could be taken into their dinghies.

The Heinkel floatplanes were originally painted white and carried Red Cross markings but representations were made to the Germans that this was in breach of the Geneva Convention, presumably because in a sense they were 'salvaging weapons of war' by picking up their airmen to fight another day. Although instances were recorded of RAF aircrew being rescued by German seaplanes an edict is believed to have been issued personally by Mr Churchill that they were to be shot down like any other combat aircraft and that this happened on at least one occasion.

In August 1940 some hasty steps were taken to set up a more formalised air-sea rescue organisation. The activities of the RAF launches were combined with those of the small naval craft under the control of local naval authorities and the twelve Lysanders 'borrowed' from Army Co-operation Command were placed under Fighter Command control to be stationed along the coastline and available to search within a twenty-mile radius of the shore. Air Sea

Rescue liaison officers were appointed to the headquarters of 10 and 11 Fighter Groups.

It was also rapidly appreciated that even in summer weather airmen in the sea needed immediate aid, particularly the precious fighter pilots still without dinghies, and three remarkable devices were evolved, each named after the RAF station where inventive officers applied their minds to the problem.

The first was the Thornaby Bag consisting of a parachute pack containing food, drink and first aid equipment and buoyed by kapok pads taken from Mae West life jackets.

The second was the Bircham Barrel (developed at RAF Bircham Newton) consisting of the cardboard tail container of a 250 lb bomb made watertight and again containing essential survival items. It was an improvement on the Thornaby Bag (which often burst on impact with the water) and could be carried on and dropped from standard bomb racks.

The third device, called Lindholme Gear, was the brainchild of Group Captain E. F. Waring, the Station Commander at Lindholme, South Yorkshire. This officer was to play a prominent part in many other aspects of rescue and his invention, after many improvements is still in use to the present day. The first Lindholme Gear consisted of an inflatable 'J' type seven-to-eight man dinghy packed in the tail unit container of a 500 lb bomb plus four supply packs utilising 250 lb containers. All five units were linked by floating rope, this feature helping downed airmen to seize the apparatus and also enabling the rescue aircraft to drop the gear in such a way that it would 'wrap itself around' survivors in the water who might be almost helpless.

The size of the central dinghy in Lindholme Gear and the equipment it carries have been constantly upgraded over 45 years with the modern equipment consisting of a Mark 9 (or nine-man) main dinghy and with the auxiliary containers reduced to two thus facilitating the quite tricky 'straddling' procedure on the part of the rescue aircraft. Lindholme Gear was originally free-dropped but various forms of restraining drogue parachutes have been added down the years.

The Gear was originally designed to fit into Hampden bombers and was perfected by early 1941. It soon became apparent that

A painting by John Norris of a Shackleton dropping Lindholme Gear. Note — although these pictures illustrate the Gear in use in the 1960s the same principles applied from about 1942 and remain to the present day. A Nimrod from Kinloss was instrumental in saving the lives of five crewmen from an Icelandic ship by dropping Lindholme Gear to them when their ship was wrecked off the Norwegian coast on Christmas Eve 1986.

almost any medium-sized aircraft could carry it and drop it. To this day every RAF Nimrod Maritime Reconnaissance aircraft carries one set at all times, those on search and rescue stand-by are loaded with two and several hundred people owe their lives to this brilliant piece of improvisation evolved in the dark days of 1940.

In its early days the Gear was normally dropped from an altitude of 120 feet at about 145 mph airspeed. In addition to food, water, first aid kits and waterproof sleeping suits, 'everhot' bags, cigarettes, matches and a pack of playing cards were included in the survival packs. The last item is believed to have been suggested personally by Mr Churchill who always had a keen eye on that factor called 'maintenance of morale'.

The early dinghies carried even in the 'heavies' of the time remained rudimentary. The original 'H' and 'J' types were redesigned to make them more stable and to enable survivors to 'sit in' on the 'floors' rather than (to use modern dinghy sailing parlance) 'sit out' on the edges from which they could easily topple when in a state of exhaustion or perhaps wounded.

In the autumn of 1940 a study was made of a captured German single-seat fighter pilot's dinghy — earlier experiments having been dropped because of technical problems — and an improved British version was developed, too late unfortunately to arrest the continuing losses of pilots dependent on their Mae Wests. (The latter device, again in a much improved form still remains the first line of defence for a downed airman in the 1980s and one imagines the lady whose name was adopted to describe it in the late 1930s would be very proud of her posterity.) A Mae West on its own will save anyone from drowning but it will not protect them much from the real enemy — *cold*.

The October 1940 aircrew losses stood at 260, a high proportion of them fighter pilots and most incurred over the sea.

In January 1941 a joint RN/RAF meeting led to the creation of a Directorate of an Air Sea Rescue Service. It was more of an organisational step forward than anything else because at that time there were no resources in the form of aeroplanes nor aircrew to spare for such a special task.

Nevertheless it was made clear at this meeting that the matter had become important enough to justify the full time appointment of an Air Commodore as Director, assisted by a Deputy Director who should be a naval officer of at least Commander rank.

Group Captain L. G. Le B. Croke, the Station Commander at RAF St Eval, Cornwall, who had shown a special interest in the subject, was appointed Director with Captain C. L. Howe, RN, as his Deputy. In all that follows it should never be forgotten that the Royal Navy played a vital part in the whole task of Air Sea Rescue and still does to the present day. Inter-Service rivalries continue, as perhaps they should, but they seldom, if ever, interfere with the ultimate task of saving life.

It should never be forgotten either that throughout World War 2 and indeed up to the present day the Royal National Lifeboat Institution has played a gallant and essential part in the rescue of 'all in peril on the sea' including many airmen. One of them, Richard Hillary, author of *The Last Enemy*, described the moment when the Margate Lifeboat crew pulled him out of the water in agony from his burns.

'Willing arms were dragging me over the side', he wrote. 'My parachute was taken off (and with such ease!); a brandy flask was pushed between my swollen lips; a voice said: "OK Joe, it's one of ours and still kicking"; and I was safe.'

Richard Hillary's rescue was one which pointed to the need for search aircraft to supplement the work of the surface craft. The Margate Lifeboat had been misdirected by well-meaning shore watchers and had been searching in the wrong place for three hours. The crew were just about to turn for home when one of them spotted Hillary's parachute as it rose on the swell simultaneously with their boat.

Perhaps one of the most significant advances of all was made in July 1941 when three Walrus amphibians 'owned' by Coastal Command were authorised for use as rescue aircraft. This remarkable little aeroplane, originally designed under the type name Seagull V by R. J. Mitchell of Spitfire fame to meet a Royal Australian Air Force specification, had been in Fleet Air Arm

A sight that gladdened many a downed airman's heart. A Walrus 'hove-to' and picking up a survivor *(Imperial War Museum)*.

service for several years and its potential as a rescuer had been marked down in 1940. All those in service were, however, then still urgently needed for Fleet spotter/reconnaissance duties, being able to operate by catapult from battleships and cruisers. The 'RAF proper', as opposed to the peacetime Fleet Air Arm, had nevertheless retained a few.

After the urgent requirement for some form of amphibian for the rescue service had become apparent the Navy released six more Walrus which were operated by Fighter Command from August 1941, some still flown by Fleet Air Arm crews. As a later chapter will show the Walrus, affectionately known in the Navy as 'the Shagbat', was to play a vital part in many a rescue operation both around the UK coasts and much further afield, including Australian waters where many aircraft of the type retained the Seagull V designation.

By September 1941 it became possible to form four composite Air Sea Rescue Squadrons, Nos 275, 276, 277 and 278, equipped initially with 24 Lysanders and nine Walrus and located at Valley (Anglesey), Colerne, Stapleford Tawney and Coltishall — the first and last of these stations remaining important search and rescue bases in the modern helicopter age.

Throughout 1941 various programmes were launched to expand and improve the fleets of both RAF High Speed Rescue Launches and of RN rescue craft. Larger and faster boats were built although up to

February of that year production was only running at the rate of about two vessels per month. Available resources always had to be measured against the Admiralty's requirement for combat craft. By July 1941 there were still only 27 High Speed Launches in service but the deficiency was to some extent being filled by the building of an extra forty RAF 'pinnaces' — sixty-foot diesel-engined boats of medium speed and capable of a wide variety of duties plus 21 extra seaplane tenders, forty-footers which could be used for inshore rescue work in moderate sea conditions.

Although help in the High Speed Launch building programme was sought in the United States and South Africa, the production

A Walrus exercising with a naval launch *(IWM)*.

programme was partly limited because of the shortage of suitable engines of types also urgently needed for aircraft. Nevertheless the percentages of successful rescues continued to rise from the 1940's optimistic figure of twenty per cent to 35 per cent in the first four months after the creation of the Directorate.

With the invasion threat past and the centre of gravity of RAF operations switching to the North Sea and the Atlantic the need for better 'deep search' facilities calling for longer range aircraft became obvious. This was met initially by the allocation of two squadrons of Coastal Command Hudsons equipped with ASV (Air-to-Surface Vessel) radar and the extension of the Lysander and Walrus search ranges from twenty to forty miles offshore.

Authority was given at the turn of 1941-42 for the formation of No 279 Air Sea Rescue Squadron at Bircham Newton and No 280 at Thorney Island, the first to be equipped with Hudsons and the second temporarily at least with Ansons. Both types of aircraft were capable of carrying out relatively deep search operations and of giving direct assistance by dropping Lindholme Gear. No 279 Squadron became operational in March 1942 and No 280 in June.

In spite of these improvements the problem remained of aircrew being able to survive in winter temperatures in open dinghies long enough for surface vessels to reach them and inventive minds began turning toward some form of lifeboat which could be dropped by aircraft which would provide reasonable shelter from the elements and perhaps equally importantly enable survivors to at least begin a journey to safety themselves.

Although much credit has quite rightly been given to the famous yachtsman Uffa Fox for the design of the airborne lifeboat, others were closely involved and, it might be claimed, preceded him. Back in early 1940 the then Air Vice-Marshal A. T. Harris as AOC No 5 Group envisaged a glider type boat which could be towed to the scene of a ditching, alighted to shed its wings and tailplane and then motored back to base with a 10 hp engine. Technical problems and a shortage of glider pilots made the idea impracticable and in modern parlance it was 'binned'. Another scheme for a 32-ft motor boat which could be dropped from a Hampden was discussed in 1940 but abandoned after a substantial amount of experimental work.

Even earlier, much earlier in fact, a remarkable aviator of the name of Noel Pemberton-Billing, the founder and namer of the firm called 'Supermarine' (meaning above the water in contrast to 'submarine' meaning below it) offered for sale a 'Flying Lifeboat'. This was to be a machine which after alighting could shed its wings and tail and then become a surface craft. An illustrated advertisement of this device appeared in the Royal Aero Club Year Book of 1914.

Group Captain Waring, the inventor of the Lindholme Gear, also had the idea of a motor lifeboat which could be dropped by parachute. He continued to work on the idea when he was posted from Lindholme to the Air Ministry in September 1941 and contacted a Lieutenant Robb, RNVR, who was an expert boat builder. The latter set about making drawings. Their first plan was for a wooden boat about 20 ft long fitted with sails, oars and an engine and capable of carrying up to seven survivors.

The first problem encountered was that the boat would drift rapidly downwind out of the reach of the survivors, particularly if the parachutes remained deployed. This was overcome by the fitting of a rocket-fired weighted drogue, or sea anchor, to the bows to hold the boat into wind; and of an automatic parachute release devised by Mr Raymond Quilter of the GQ Parachute Company.

The next problem of keeping the boat upright on impact with the water was solved by providing buoyancy chambers which would inflate on the way down as the opening parachutes activated the valves of carbon dioxide bottles. The last requirement was to provide a means for distressed airmen to get aboard and this was met by installing more rockets which would fire out on either side 200-ft lengths of floating rope.

These fundamental devices were fitted to a series of Marks of Airborne Lifeboats, the last of which remained operational until the 1950s and which were responsible for the saving of several hundred lives, many of them the lives of airmen under enemy fire or while afloat in the midst of enemy minefields.

In January 1942 authority was given for a contract to be placed with Uffa Fox and his firm for the building of a fleet of such boats. Although they eventually became known as the 'Uffa Fox Airborne Lifeboats' and the great yachtsman put much thought and ingenuity into the eventual designs, less than fair credit has ever been given to Group Captain Waring and Lieutenant Robb.

Tests with the 'Airborne Lifeboat Mark I' in July and August of 1942 were successful and a production contract was placed in September. In preparing the detailed design Uffa Fox had assumed that Hudsons would be the 'carriers'. At about that time, however, a decision was made to replace the Hudson in the deep search air-sea rescue role with the Vickers Warwick; a medium bomber design which had proved somewhat unsatisfactory for its first designated role, and this caused some confusion. The Warwick was really an 'up-gunned' Wellington.

Perhaps fortunately it was found that No 279 Squadron's Hudsons could remain operational until at least early 1943 so provision was made for the building of 24 boats suitable to be carried by them while preparations went on for an improved version to be fitted to Warwicks. While the Warwick emerged as the prime Airborne Lifeboat carrier of World War 2, such boats were fitted

A successful Airborne Lifeboat drop. The bow and stern buoyancy compartments have inflated and the parachutes are about to be automatically cut clear *(Jim Forrest)*.

to many other types including at least one Fleet Air Arm Barracuda and to several Fortresses. At the end of the war and into the 1950s the Mark III boats were carried by Lancasters and by some prototype Shackletons.

The potential of flying boats as rescuers was obviously appreciated at an early stage of the entire art, but for some time only the gallant little Walrus (actually 'amphibian flying boats') had the opportunity to demonstrate the potential. Coastal Command's growing fleets of Sunderlands and Catalinas were, however, destined to be

Lockheed Hudson with Airborne Lifeboat. Hudsons were the first American-built aircraft to see operational service in World War 2. Military versions of the Lockheed 14 Super Electra, they were powered either by Wright Cyclones or Pratt and Whitney Twin Wasps. More than 2,000 were delivered and they carried out numerous Coastal Command and overseas duties including lifeboat carrying *(RAF)*.

instrumental in the saving of hundreds, possibly thousands, of lives either directly or indirectly.

Because of the reasons outlined at the beginning of this chapter 'complete' rescues by flying boats, which were able to alight and take off again from mid-ocean, were comparatively rare; but many were in fact achieved and will be related later. Leaving those episodes aside perhaps the biggest contribution made towards life-saving in World War 2 lay in the assistance flying boats gave to the survivors of torpedoed ships — by *finding* them, reporting their positions, dropping aids to them and guiding surface rescue vessels to them.

Towards the end of the war the flying boats of Coastal Command were being supported by (and were eventually to be supplanted by) 'Very Long Range' landplanes such as Liberators, Halifaxes and Fortresses and they too played a vital part in the whole search and rescue operations over the Atlantic and in other sea war zones.

Much earlier the close-range search and rescue operations were assisted by two other aircraft type — the Boulton and Paul Defiant and, perhaps a bit surprisingly, the omniferous Spitfire. By 1942 spares for the

Lysanders were becoming difficult to obtain and the aircraft type had acquired a very special role indeed, the dropping and recovery of clandestine agents on the European mainland. The Defiant was another 'unsatisfactory' type in its designated role as a two-seater night fighter so some became available as air-sea rescue 'spotters'. The availability of some of these aircraft made it possible to form yet another Air Sea Rescue Squadron, No 281 in March 1942. The Defiants only had limited success however, even in this alternative role.

In early 1943 it became possible to bring the Spitfire into the air-sea rescue scenario. By this time many rescues had to be carried out in the midst of both air and surface battles and the advantage of having a rescue aeroplane which could fight its way in and out of such situations was clearly attractive. Again inventive minds went to work and it was found possible to fit equipment consisting of a 'L' type dinghy, emergency rations, water and first aid kit into the flare chutes of Mark 1 and Mark 2 Spitfires and for all of them to be fired out to descend in the water near the survivor. The 'packages' were linked by floating rope.

The early air-sea rescue described in detail at the beginning of this chapter emphasised

A Boulton Paul Defiant. Powered by Rolls Royce Merlin III or XX according to Mark. Max speed about 300 mph *(RAF Museum)*.

the importance of communications, on that occasion provided by pigeons. Pigeons remained in official RAF service until 1943 with many volunteer 'fanciers' operating lofts as members of the National Pigeon Service.

In February 1942 a bird known as 'Winkie' played an important role in a successful rescue. A Beaufort from Leuchars failed to return after having given its position as 150 miles east of Aberdeen. Two pigeons were aboard the aircraft, one of which escaped without a message during the ditching, the other being despatched in the approved manner with a position report on its leg. Only the 'truant' without a message reached its loft but its owner was able to calculate from its condition its estimated time in the air and adding the factor that birds do not fly at night worked out that the aircraft had ditched about fifty miles closer to Leuchars than the last signalled position. The search area was therefore adjusted and the Beaufort's dinghy was sighted by a Hudson. Two High Speed Launches and a Walrus were despatched and four survivors brought ashore 24 hours after their ditching.

In the summer of 1943 when the RAF Home Commands were discussing the abolition of the pigeon service, a Baltimore ditched in the Mediterranean 100 miles from base. An SOS had been sent and a DF fix obtained but in poor visibility an aircraft search was unsuccessful. The crew, who had taken their pigeon containers into the dinghy, found one drowned, the other very wet. The second pigeon was dried out and released and reached base with a message 'Crew safe in dinghy 10 degrees W. of Tocra'. The next morning a launch found them and brought them in unscathed.

Just before the Pigeon Service was finally stood down a Catalina flying to the west of the Shetlands had to alight in bad weather and was damaged. A pigeon reached the aircraft's base at Sullom Voe during the evening with a location message. A wireless message was broadcast telling the Catalina crew to use their dinghy transmitter and a faint signal was picked up. The flying boat was located by searching surface craft just before midnight, the crew rescued and the aircraft abandoned.

Many people in fact regretted the decision to close down the pigeon service because it had taken some time to develop satisfactory emergency wireless transmitters which were sufficiently rugged and reliable and small and light enough to be carried in dinghies — it was, of course, before the age of transistors and miniaturisation.

If a pilot or wireless operator had time to transmit an SOS or 'M'aidez' (Mayday) with an accurate position and then send out a carrier wave on which a DF bearing could be taken there was a fair chance of rescue. Early attempts to aid searchers included the use of balloons and kites, the adoption (based on the German example) of bright yellow life jackets and the provision of marker dye and improved distress flares.

Experiments began on the design of a dinghy transmitter in 1941 but after the capture of a German (NS 2) set the British prototype was scrapped and in September that year production ordered of 2,000 modified versions of the latter to be known as Type 1333. A further 8,000 were ordered in January 1942. These sets operated on the 500 kilocycle International Distress Frequency.

Many difficulties were encountered and it was found initially that the set could not be installed permanently in a dinghy but had to be carried loose in the aircraft. It was later recorded that in 95 per cent of ditchings it was left behind. By July 1942 only sixteen had been produced and an order was placed for 1,000 American sets, designated SCR 578, which were in fact exact reproductions of the German NS 2s. In the event the American sets proved superior to the T 1333s and 12,000 of them were delivered to Britain.

Partly because of the difficulty of packing either type into dinghies, thought was given to the provision of a device which would show up on a search aircraft's ASV radar. One unsatisfactory idea was to fit dinghies with metal 'flags' on telescopic masts — a forerunner of the modern transponder or radar reflector. Later a device code-named 'WALTER' was evolved consisting of a battery and a seven-foot telescopic mast with an oscillator and a horizontal dipole on top. It weighed only twenty ounces, the battery had a theoretical twenty-hour life and it could be packed into even a one-man dinghy, albeit at the expense of sails. Production of WALTER did not, however, begin until January 1944.

A Mark II Spitfire. Some aircraft of this type were used for air-sea rescue work, being able to 'fight their own way' in and out and drop survival gear from flare racks *(Bruce Robertson)*.

(In spite of its crudeness and questionable efficiency WALTER was to be the progenitor of a whole series of locator beacons culminating in the present equipment not much bigger than a cigarette packet, permanently fitted to aircrew life jackets, operating automatically on ejection and enabling a helicopter or even a large search aircraft such as a Nimrod to pinpoint a human head in mid-ocean on a dark night.)

As the war went on numerous improvements were made to all the items of equipment mentioned above. For some time, however, the specialist air-sea rescue squadrons tended to remain poor relations when it came to the allocation of aircraft.

Airborne lifeboats were upgraded through the Mark 1A, Mark 2 and Mark 3 stages; many more even faster and more seaworthy High Speed Launches came into service, mounting their own defensive armament; dinghies were improved and perhaps most importantly *skills* improved in the light of experience by both rescuers and survivors.

The whole matter of a successful rescue clearly depended not only on the skills and determination of the searchers and rescuers but upon those of the survivors themselves. There is a certain amount of evidence that some Allied airmen, particularly the often inexperienced Bomber Command crews, did not take the subject of survival as seriously as they might have done. One incident recorded in February 1942 showed that five complete aircrews were lost because they had failed to carry out the correct wireless procedure before ditching.

Many other examples were logged of instances where crews fumbled their escape procedures, leaving hatches open which should have been closed, others closed which should have been open, and left transmitters behind when under a proper drill someone would have been capable of getting them into dinghies.

Before casting too much adverse judgment on such lapses it should perhaps be remembered that Bomber Command crews in particular lived under very special stresses. Many inevitably had superstitions and perhaps the familiar 'it-won't-happen-to-me' syndrome applied. Training and practice in ditching and escape procedures had to be carried out in their precious hours of relaxation and sleep between the dawn of one day and the dusk of the same and many felt they had more important things to do with those hours left to them. Who could blame them if they felt ditching and survival drill to be a bore?

However, many aircrews and aircraft captains took a different view, perhaps especially those who served in Coastal Command and who saw the cruel sea constantly. They — and to be fair, many Bomber Command crews — studied and practised ditching and survival drills religiously whenever they had the chance and perhaps significantly several of them have been able to write to this author in 1986 recording their experiences.

Bryan Turnbull, Royal New Zealand Air Force, who was the captain of a Hudson of 206 Squadron in 1941 and later of a Liberator of 120 Squadron and whose close friends were involved in a classic rescue to be described later, wrote to me in 1986: 'As a Coastal Command pilot my flying was almost all over the sea so you may understand that I spent a lot of time getting prepared for an unscheduled ducking. I always enjoyed having pigeons with me and set great store by my Mae West with torch and whistle, compass buttons, morphine and needles, compressed food, foreign money, and large sharp pocket knife.

'We carried three automatic release dinghies in our 120 Squadron Liberators, plus a large one inside the fuselage complete with pedal generator and radio, a kite to raise an aerial and a cover to keep the dinghy dry.

'My crew swam with me almost every day in the enormous thermal pool in Reykjavik (Iceland) and practised life-saving exercises. On almost every trip I flew at fifty feet or less to keep my hand in, just as I occasionally feathered a couple of propellers for practice.

'Every member of my crew learned to fly straight and level, and all wore wool and leather clothing. Fire and ditching were our greatest threats outside the angry bullet, so we willingly took precautions.

'From personal experience you have my assurance that the sight of dozens of submariners, alive or dead, bobbing about in an oil slick in mid-Atlantic; of a large ship turned turtle; of a tanker aflame from stem to

stern, is enough to inspire aircrew to the belief that air-sea rescue, like charity, begins at home.'

At high level the need for more training in survival was appreciated and in March 1942 an Air Sea Rescue Officer was appointed to every operational station of the RAF. By that time it had become clear that the best hope of survival over the sea (usually the inhospitable North Sea at that stage of the war) lay in ditching rather than parachuting, especially so far as bomber crews were concerned. An official report said: 'The task of the Station Rescue Officer was a formidable one as he had to arouse the interest of his audience, when frequently he had not the up-to-date knowledge nor practical experience which would make his lectures and demonstrations convincing'. (What that passage really meant was that the efforts of a young 'wingless wonder' doing his best, had little effect upon a cynical and pretty tired audience of mixed officer and NCO aircrews from Halifaxes and Lancasters who just wanted to go back to bed again for an hour or two or perhaps date a

A Sikorsky 'Hoverfly I' (R-4 in United States parlance). Some USAAF R-4s carried out rescues in Burma from 1944 onwards but the British-owned aircraft, of which this is one, never became operational in World War 2 although a number were evaluated, mainly by the Fleet Air Arm, whose officers foresaw many roles for helicopters in the future. The R-4, or Hoverfly, was the first practical helicopter available to the Allies. The Germans had advanced much further but were not exploiting their skills and knowledge in this field of aviation. The Hoverfly I/R-4 was powered by a single 180 hp Warner piston engine. Its loaded weight was 2,530 lb and its maximum speed 82 mph.

The effects upon body and mind of being in a dinghy for five days are written on the features of this member of a bomber crew at the moment of final rescue by an RAF ASR launch. He was one of only two survivors *(RAF)*.

WAAF or perhaps consume a pint in a local pub before the next raid.)

A sharp warning about the inadequacy of aircrew training in survival was issued in February 1943 when the Deputy Director of Air Sea Rescue stated that out of 1,761 aircrews who came down in the sea in the last six months of 1942 1,116 lives were lost — 66 per cent of the total. He said he was convinced that one of the major problems affecting this depressing figure was the standard of training of aircrew *and of the maintenance personnel responsible for rescue equipment.*

As a step towards rectification of this defect a School of Air Sea Rescue was established at Blackpool in May 1943. It ran two-week courses, each accommodating twenty officers; could use RAF marine craft based at nearby Fleetwood for exercises and could call on two Ansons. During its first seven-month existence the School trained 520 officers in rescue procedures and more than 3,000 Safety Equipment Assistants. Nevertheless the aircrew losses at sea reached a new high in 1943 with 1,188 lost or believed lost out of a total of 5,466 airmen who had ditched or parachuted to apparent safety. The rescue

services helped in the saving of 1,684 lives, just under a third of the total 'in distress'.

When the first United States Army Air Force crews arrived in Britain in the spring and summer of 1942 it was soon discovered that they were woefully short of knowledge about ditching procedures and survival at sea, all their previous training and experience having been conducted over land with 'baling out' by parachute accepted as a standard procedure in the case of any emergency in the air. Joint arrangements for search and rescue cover between the RAF and the USAAF were quickly made and the American bomber crews proved themselves willing learners in the arts of ditching and survival.

Some statistics seem to show that a much higher proportion of American bomber crews survived in the sea than did their counterparts in the RAF during the height of the bombing offensive against Germany. Any interpretation of such statistics should, however, take into account the facts that the majority of American bomber aircrews in distress ditched in daylight, making the searches for them and the despatch of aid, that much easier than in the cases of RAF night bomber crews going down in the middle of the North Sea. Nevertheless, during August 1943 the percentage of aircrew saved from the

For some fairly obvious reasons the RAF's standard inflatable life jacket was nicknamed at an early stage as a 'Mae West'. The title stuck and for many years has become official terminology. Here is the lady who gave her name to one of the most valuable life-saving aids ever invented. One imagines she has always liked this contribution to her immortality.

US Eighth Air Force was sixty per cent. On 6 and 7 September 1943 118 out of 121 aircrew in distress were saved. These figures inevitably worsened during the winter months.

One intriguing factor emerging was that the British version of the Mae West life jacket turned out to be superior to that supplied to US aircrews which did not have an effective neck collar to keep the survivor's head out of the water. British versions were gladly supplied to the USAAF notwithstanding the nationality of the lady who gave her name to the device.

By the end of World War 2 in 1945 more than 13,000 lives had been saved by the British Air Sea Rescue Service, about 8,000 of them aircrew. In 'Home Waters' alone nearly 6,000 airmen had been rescued. Impressive though these figures are it must still be remembered that they only represented about forty per cent of those lost at sea and of course the Service had its encouraging and discouraging periods.

Some remarkable totals were recorded — in July 1943 139 out of 196 Fortress aircrews ditched were saved. On one day 78 out of 80. During the Dieppe Raid in 1942 106 aircraft were lost but only eighty airmen reported dead or missing.

One particularly poignant 'statistic' records the finding of eight British fighter pilots dead from exposure in their dinghies on one day. Perhaps one of the greatest forward steps taken was the fitting of little sails to fighter pilots' one-man dinghies so that at least they could feel they were 'going-home' and not just drifting helplessly.

As the war progressed other techniques were being developed to help those in distress on mountains, in jungles and deserts. In Burma, in 1944 a little group of USAAF pilots began rescuing wounded British soldiers and some of their own fellow airmen from under the noses of the Japanese with strange little aircraft, nicknamed by them 'Eggbeaters' and officially styled Sikorsky R-4 helicopters. They were to open up a whole new phase of the art of saving life from the air which will be related later.

Against this general background some of the detailed stories of life saving during World War 2 can now be told.

Chapter Two
Second World War:
Rescues by combinations of surface vessels and aircraft

The Second World War incidents described in this chapter have been selected to demonstrate the co-operative effort called for from many agencies to bring about successful rescues — from the specialised RAF marine craft, from RN vessels ranging in size from Motor Launches to frigates and destroyers, from the RNLI boats, sometimes from civilian craft (not always officially 'on our side') and from the searching and 'direct-aid' aircraft. These incidents can only be regarded as a cross-section of hundreds.

Few records were kept of rescue operations until after the formation of the ASR Directorate in February 1941, so that the details of the many carried out during the Battle of Britain and the beginning of the bombing offensive against Germany can only be traced through such personal reminiscences as were committed to paper during those hectic days when most concerned had more urgent things to do.

A very early, and typical, rescue was recorded briefly in a Ministry of Information booklet published in 1942. It read: 'A Spitfire received several hits in the petrol tanks. It became uncontrollable and flung the pilot out.

'The next thing he remembers is falling quite clear from the machine and unhurt. He pulled the ripcord when at 28,000 ft and, stimulated by a recent discussion in the Mess on how long it would take to fall to ground level from that height, he carefully timed his descent.

'It took 24 1/2 minutes. While in the air he took both his boots off and dropped them one after the other to help in estimating the final hundred feet or so of drop.

'He released his parachute harness as his feet touched the water; his "Mae West" had been punctured and could not be inflated.' (This incident took place during the Battle of Britain before fighter pilots were provided with the 'K' type of dinghy.) However his parachute had been seen from land and a motor launch picked him up after he had been in the water for two hours. This un-named pilot was one of the fortunate twenty per cent at best to have baled out during the early stages of the Battle of Britain and to have been rescued.

The following account by Pilot Officer Stevenson of No 74 Squadron, dated 11 August 1940, appeared in Denis Richards's history of the Royal Air Force. He became engaged in a battle with a large force of Me 109s north of Dover and as some of them attacked him he later recorded: 'There was a popping noise and my control column became useless. I found myself doing a vertical dive getting faster and faster. I pulled the hood back. I got my head out of the cockpit and the slipstream tore the rest of me clean out of the machine.

'My trouser leg and both shoes were torn off. I saw my machine crash into the sea a mile off Deal. It took me twenty minutes to come down. I had been drifted eleven miles out to sea. One string of my parachute did not come undone and I was dragged along by my left leg at ten miles an hour with my head underneath the water. After three minutes I was almost unconscious when the string came undone. I got my breath back and started swimming. There was a heavy sea running.

'After one and a half hours an MTB came to look for me. I fired my revolver at it. It went out of sight but came back. I changed magazines and fired all my shots over it. It heard my shots and I kicked up a foam in the water. It then picked me up and took me to

Dover.' (This account, using an economy of language and short sentences could perhaps be regarded as a model of 'reportage'. Superlatives are not needed when describing such an experience.)

Another item in the Ministry of Information booklet recorded the experiences of a Hurricane pilot who, having run out of ammunition, was shot down in mid-Channel. This report, although undated, obviously refers to a later period, probably in early 1941, when single-seat fighter pilots had been supplied with dinghies. It read: 'I stayed in as long as I could but finally seeing flames and feeling uncomfortably hot I decided to get out'.

When this Hurricane pilot hit the water the shroud lines of his parachute fell on top of him as there was no wind. His dinghy pack sank but remained attached to him.

'I had great difficulty in pulling up the dinghy because I was entangled in the parachute shroud lines' he reported, well before hundreds of other ditched pilots encountered a similar problem, some of them in quite recent years. He eventually got the dinghy free and blew it up. 'I could see no land either side of me and started paddling with my hands towards the English coast using the sun as a guide.

'After about half an hour I saw a biplane approaching from France at sea level escorted by six single-seater aircraft. They flew over me and I presumed that they were Me 109s escorting a Heinkel floatplane. I at once got out of the dinghy and made myself scarce in the water about twenty yards away.

'The whole formation then turned back towards the French coast. In the meantime I had seen a Lysander several miles away. Presently it came towards me and I saw that it was escorted by some Spitfires.

'The next thing that happened was that they attacked some Me 109s at about 3,000 ft, one of which went into the sea. A moment later a number of Hurricanes arrived and joined in the fray.

'Some of the Spitfires attacked some more '109s and also the Heinkel floatplane which fell into the sea and blew up, leaving a column of black smoke.

'I also saw a Spitfire go into the sea; it flicked over on its back just above the water and went straight in. I did not see anyone bale out. Soon afterwards I was alone again and continued to paddle towards England until I could see the coastline.

'Then I saw two High Speed Launches on patrol but they did not see me. One of them came fairly close and I managed to attract its attention by splashing and shouting for help for I had no whistle. The launch came up. I was hauled aboard and taken to Dover none the worse for my adventures.'

The shooting down of the Heinkel seaplane, presumably a German rescue aircraft, described above does of course, pose many questions about 'chivalry' which could be argued about for ever.

Squadron Leader Laurie Edwards, Royal New Zealand Air Force, was among a handful of Allied airmen to be picked up from the sea by German floatplanes, but in his case his 'benefactor' was not a rescue aircraft and certainly no chivalry was involved. The Anson *(K6183)* of 206 Squadron which he was piloting over the North Sea soon after the outbreak of war in September 1939 was attacked by a formation of Arado seaplanes. The then Pilot Officer Edwards had a co-pilot/navigator, a wireless operator and an air gunner aboard — the last a ground crew airman who 'had jumped aboard' to earn an extra sixpence for the day's flying as aircrew under the current rules.

All aboard were hit by machine-gun fire and both engines were set on fire. Laurie, the least seriously hit with wounds to the head and feet and face burns was the only one to survive the ditching.

One of the Arados alighted and he was grabbed aboard. During the flight back to Nordeney in the Friesian Isles one of the Arado crew covered him with a pistol. He was then imprisoned in a 7 x 7-ft cell for the night in spite of his injuries. He was later visited by a doctor and interrogated by the Arado aircrew (without any result) before transfer to a PoW Camp with the doubtful distinction of becoming the first prisoner taken during World War 2.

Some examples of chivalry displayed by the German air sea rescue services have been recorded including one in which a Luftwaffe aircraft 'pointed' an RAF launch towards survivors in a dinghy for whom they were searching and which might well have been shot down for its pains had the launch's guns not jammed at a critical moment.

In his book *Years of Command* Lord Douglas of Kirtleside, earlier Air Marshal Sholto Douglas, revealed that a discreet wireless channel was kept open between the two sides when he was AOC in C of Fighter Command so that the RAF could tell the Germans when there were aircrew in the sea off the French coast and *vice versa* when Germans were down off the English shoreline.

This channel, which Lord Douglas said was not generally known about 'even to high authority,' was used when Douglas Bader was shot down leaving one of his artificial legs badly bent in the wreckage of his aircraft after baling out. The Germans offered safe conduct to an aircraft dropping a spare leg. This was declined and the leg was dropped by a Blenheim during a raid on St Omer. The channel was used again to notify the Germans that the drop had been made and an acknowledgement of receipt came back

promptly. (Meanwhile the Germans had repaired Group Captain Bader's original leg and he had temporarily escaped with it.)

On 21 June 1941 a Czech fighter pilot engaged by Me 109s was hit eight miles south of Folkestone. He tried to reach the English coast but realising he was going to fall short made wireless contact with his base. He made a good ditching, got clear of his aircraft and was able to inflate his one-man dinghy. After half an hour a Lysander escorted by four Spitfires appeared overhead. He waved to them, they saw him, circled him and returned to base. Only fifteen *minutes* later an RAF Rescue Launch picked him up and took him back to Dover.

An important feature of this rescue, appertaining to many others, was that the pilot, being a Czech, was anxious to fly as far away as possible from enemy-occupied territory before baling out. He would probably NOT have been given the full courtesies of a Prisoner-of-War.

The 1942 Ministry of Information booklet included this account of a Polish Spitfire

An aircrew survivor being brought aboard an RAF Rescue Launch *circa* 1940 *(RAF)*.

pilot's rescue, which down the years cannot be improved upon and is reproduced verbatim.

'I dived behind one of the Messerschmitts and opened fire at 200 yd. But I did not see another Messerschmitt coming in on my right. Suddenly my windscreen was covered with oil.'

The Sergeant Pilot was then half way between Lille and the Channel. His engine began to run more and more roughly as the oil drained out of it, and about eight miles out from the French coast it stopped. He decided to land in the sea, for by that time he was too late to bale out.

'I hit the water with my tail and then my Spitfire leaned forward and sank like a stone', the pilot's report said. 'I went down with it. Something struck me underneath the eyes so that I could not see. When I opened them it was very dark. I got out through the top of the cockpit, but it was very hard to do so because of the parachute strapped to me on which I was sitting.

'Before I got out I went down very deep. I could not breathe. I thought it was finish with my life.'

On reaching the surface the pilot succeeded in disengaging his parachute harness. His report went on to say: 'The sea was quiet. I pulled the string of the dinghy, opened the bottle of gas and waited for the dinghy to blow up, which it did very easily.

'I tried three times to climb on to it but it kept shooting up in the water because I had forgotten to push it forward so as to fill the water pocket in its nose. When I remembered to do this I climbed in easily.'

It was then about a quarter to one in the afternoon of a fine sunny Wednesday in June 1941. The pilot was warm and his clothing soon dried. He tried to paddle towards England with his hands, but could make little progress. His hopes of rescue were, however, high. Fighter sweeps were going on at frequent intervals and he felt sure someone would see him.

The afternoon wore on. He could hear aircraft at frequent intervals going and returning, but he could not see them. They were too high or perhaps it was because of his eyes which were injured and bleeding. At about 8 pm in the evening he made up his mind that he was in the dinghy for the night.

The sea got up. Soon he was very cold and the dinghy shipped much water which he baled out with his hands. The storm subsided at about 2 am in the morning.

'All night I lay shivering, waiting for the sun to rise. Presently the sky turned red. It was very nice. When the sun was high I took off all my clothes, though this was not easy to do in the dinghy, and dried them. They took two or three hours to dry. When they were ready I put them on and tried to sleep.'

He dozed, with long waking intervals, throughout that summer day. Once more aircraft passed over his head, but they could not see him nor he them. Towards evening he saw a German float boat of the kind moored by the enemy in the Channel to provide those who are shot down with a temporary refuge in the sea. It was too far off and he could not reach it. The second night came down and once again the sea got up, subsiding as on the first night an hour before dawn. Once more the pilot was soaked and spent the morning in drying his clothes. He still felt confident of rescue. 'All that day aircraft were flying to and from France and I felt sure someone was bound to see me, and then what a surprise it would be for my friends. No one did see me.'

A 7 o'clock in the evening he saw another float boat; this one was British. He left his dinghy, tied it to his Mae West and began to swim towards the boat. The distance was 800 yd. He had not the strength to reach it and climbed once more into his dinghy as the sun was setting. He had now been two days in the sea in a rubber craft the length of a man's body with a freeboard of about eight inches.

The third night was a repetition of the other two with rough seas and the added discomfort of rain. Once more when dawn broke the pilot took off his clothes and spent the morning drying them. He did not feel hungry but his thirst was terrible. 'There was plenty of water all round me in the Channel but it was too sour to drink.' He spent the day thinking about the Sergeants' Mess and the beer he drank in it with his friends and how he was apt to grumble at the food, which was English and not what he liked.

Throughout the morning of the fourth day more sweeps went over him towards France. By this time he was beginning to think that unless some aircraft flew low he would not be seen. A number of Blenheims went out about 1 o'clock in the afternoon. 'On their return their engines had a different voice because they were low. They passed some 600 yd to my right but nobody saw me. Presently another Blenheim came flying from France with a Hurricane escorting it. They came straight for me very low. Then they both made a turn and I knew they had seen me.

'The Blenheim went on but the Hurricane flew round and round me. I saw its number painted on it and knew it to be one of the Polish Squadron.'

Forty minutes later a Lysander, escorted by three Spitfires, was over him and within an hour an air-sea rescue launch was alongside his dinghy. 'I thought I could climb on board but found I couldn't, so two of the crew pulled me up.

'The officer was about to give me a glass of rum when he asked me when I had had my last food. I said: "Wednesday". He said: "Good God, today is Sunday", and I said "Yes" so he gave me only water with just a spot of rum in it.'

They made him lie down, gave him a piece of dry bread, then a slice with butter and jam on it and presently a glass of water followed by one of rum and water mixed. They landed

him at a Kent port where he was taken to hospital. An hour later that same launch had rescued another Polish airman who was put in the next bed. 'He was pleased to see me but told me that all my kit had been divided up among my friends.'

This Polish Sergeant Pilot was on operational duties again within a fortnight of his rescue.

On 21 June 1941 Squadron Leader Stanford Tuck (then on his way to becoming one of the World War 2 'ace' fighter pilots) was attacked by three Me 109s off the Dutch coast. He shot two of the enemy down and damaged the third but his own aircraft was damaged and he baled out some four miles off the Suffolk coast. He made a classic descent but had some difficulty ripping the cover off his dinghy and inflating it. A Lysander passed overhead and a barge whose skipper had seen him bale out steered towards him. Squadron Leader Tuck paddled towards the barge and climbed aboard it. Shortly afterwards a naval launch, guided by the Lysander, came out and collected him.

On the same day a Hurricane pilot separated from his squadron while escorting bombers over Boulogne, was attacked by Me 109s on his way back across the Channel. He

A ditched Whitley with the crew getting clear aboard their dinghy *(RAF Museum)*.

baled out when his aircraft caught fire and after some difficulty extricating himself from entangled parachute lines, boarded his dinghy. Seeing no land either side of him he started paddling with his hands towards home, using the sun as his guide. After half an hour he saw a Heinkel 59 float plane and an Me 109 and dived out of his dinghy to seek concealment in the water.

After they passed he got back aboard his dinghy again and resumed paddling towards the English coast. A Lysander flew overhead escorted by some Spitfires which turned to attack some Me 109s. Some Hurricanes appeared and joined in the fray; a Spitfire and an Me 109 were shot down into the sea. The downed Hurricane pilot watched the scene with some fascination but then continued his paddling. Several RAF High Speed Launches then appeared, apparently alerted to look for the pilot of the downed Spitfire. The Hurricane pilot attracted the attention of one of the launches by splashing and shouting and was taken into Dover. He is reported to have maintained rather volubly that if he had been left alone he would have made the shore by nightfall anyway.

The only recorded successful RAF rescue involving a 'Cuckoo' rescue buoy, took place in late October 1942 when Flying Officer G. G. Galwey, Royal Australian Air Force, had to bale out of his Spitfire at low level over the Channel after a fight with a number of Fw 109s. He boarded his dinghy and was still paddling when darkness fell and he saw a flashing red light. On closing with it he realised that it was a rescue buoy and after some difficulty fighting the tide managed to make his dinghy painter fast to it. Although by then somewhat weak in the legs he managed to board it. No details are available of his final rescue but since he had described his position as being within sight of the Dover cliffs when he first baled out and the buoy should have been fitted with radio this was probably a fairly routine matter. All rescue buoys were visually inspected daily by ASR aircraft and rescue launches visited them whenever possible.

In 1941 a Whitley returning from a raid on Berlin was hit in both engines by fire from German night fighters and ditched ninety miles from the Humber estuary in the early hours of the morning. The aircraft, already on fire at the time of ditching, blew up and sank just as the crew had got clear with their

A Mark IV Blenheim. This bomber type often played a major role in search operations *(Bruce Robertson)*.

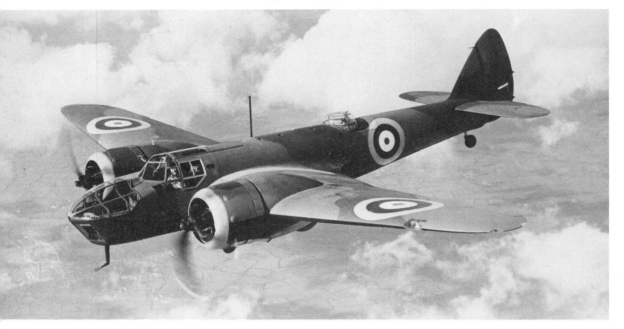

Many devices, including kites, were used to improve air-sea rescue techniques. In this training picture a 'ditched' aircrew are flying a kite to lift their emergency wireless aerial to an altitude from which its signal might be picked up *(Bruce Robertson)*.

dinghy. Unfortunately during the evacuation the dinghy turned upside down shedding most of the precious emergency stores apart from two distress flares.

For two days the crew had to cling to the inverted dinghy, two of them paddling in turn, the other two baling with shoes and an empty Very light cartridge. During the first day another Whitley located them but then lost sight of them in the high seas. The following day a Hudson spotted them and dropped supplies and flame floats. Later that evening a Hampden dropped Lindholme Gear to them and they were able to board its central dinghy. As darkness fell a Royal Air Force High Speed Launch reached them and took them into Grimsby.

One of the biggest combined life-saving efforts by the Royal Navy and the RAF, involving the use of rescue and fighter aircraft, High Speed Launches, small naval craft and a destroyer, was mounted on the night 11/12 August 1942 when a 'Leigh Light' Wellington of No 172 Squadron ditched in the Bay of Biscay. (The 'Leigh Light', a high-powered airborne searchlight, was an

important weapon in the anti-submarine war at this time.)

During this whole operation the lives of seven RAF aircrew were saved but seventeen others were lost together with three aircraft so that the 'score' was a doubtful one according to how records are kept. The tally of courage displayed, skills used and lessons learned makes it an important episode to record in any history of air-sea rescue.

The Wellington, captained by Flying Officer A. W. R. Triggs, encountered engine trouble with clouds of sparks being observed by the tail gunner, the oil pressure on one engine falling to zero. The ditching drill was carried out impeccably in total darkness, high seas and winds including the transmission of an SOS. The dinghy, however, failed to blow out of the stowage and Triggs had to prise it out with his bare hands. It then inflated and the crew of six climbed aboard. They were then constantly drenched by breaking waves and had to spend the next six hours baling continuously.

At first light they fired their only two distress flares in an unsuccessful attempt to

A Beaufighter, another operational type which frequently played a major part in rescues. Many downed aircrews owed their lives to friendly Beaufighters which circled them, fended off enemies and conveyed position signals to shore bases and rescue launches. This is a 'Beau' of 404 Squadron pictured at Banff, Scotland (*Bruce Robertson*).

A Beaufort exercising with an RAF pinnace, in 1943 (*Bruce Robertson*).

attract the attention of a Beaufighter and a Whitley which passed overhead. Nine other aircraft were sighted later in the morning but by then the Wellington crew only had a flag and a bag of fluorescine dye with which to attract attention.

Later a Whitley escorted by three Beaufighters saw them and dropped a Thornaby Bag and a spare dinghy. The former, containing a Very pistol and cartridges, was reached but the spare dinghy drifted out of reach. This Whitley was able to signal an accurate position of the dinghies on its return to base and a Sunderland was despatched with a Beaufighter escort.

Another Whitley saw the Wellington crew and cheered them mightily by Aldis-lamp signal saying 'Sunderland coming'. Sadly this Whitley was shot down with the loss of its entire crew on its way back to base.

The captain of the Sunderland from No 461 Squadron, Royal Australian Air Force, then made a gallant effort, but committed a cardinal error, which was often to be

repeated. From even a moderate height he underestimated the roughness of the sea and in particular the range of the 'swell'. As he touched down the flying boat hit a wave, bounded, hit the water and lost the starboard wingtip together with its float. A second later a starboard engine caught fire and the aircraft nosed into the sea. The Sunderland crew had time to launch one of their own dinghies but it burst open, scattering them all into the water.

The Sunderland navigator then swam towards the spare dinghy dropped earlier by the Whitley and tried to bring it towards his comrades, clinging on to the side and using his feet as 'propellers'. He was, however, rapidly exhausted and he had to clamber aboard the dinghy himself to see his comrades drown beyond his reach.

The following day search aircraft saw the 'spare' dinghy dropped by the Whitley and thought all the crashed Sunderland crew were aboard, not just the one survivor. Two more Whitleys arrived on the scene and circled the dinghies but three German Arado fighting seaplanes appeared in pursuit of them.

While all this was going on the Wellington crew lay low in their dinghy in the hope that the enemy aircraft would either not see them or think them dead. The weather had deteriorated and for two days (14 and 15 August) rescue attempts by aircraft had to be abandoned, but the destroyer HMS *Tynedale* sailed from Falmouth to help.

The Wellington crew at this stage also made an attempt to sail for home using the dinghy cover, their telescopic mast and bandages from their first-aid kit to improvise a rig which gave them some progress when the winds were favourable.

On the fourth day (16 August) two Beaufighters appeared overhead and signalled 'Contact other dinghy. Injured man aboard'. The Wellington crew began paddling over the 1,000 yd which separated the two boats and then a Hudson dropped a set of Lindholme Gear to them. The Lindholme dinghy landed upside-down but the Wellington crew managed to right it and tie it to their own. After *five hours* of paddling they reached the sole Sunderland survivor and tied all three dinghies together.

During that day HMS *Tynedale* continued her search, sometimes escorted by

Flying Officer Triggs and his crew waving to a rescue launch towards the end of their long ordeal.

Beaufighters and accompanied by Royal Navy fast patrol boats and by RAF High Speed Launches. One Beaufighter shot down a Ju 88.

Early in the morning of 17 August three Hudsons and two Beaufighters were overhead and other friendly aircraft were in the vicinity. A Beaufighter sighted an enemy motor launch escorted by three Arados and 'discouraged' it from coming closer. A Hudson signalled the position of the dinghies to some of the searching RN launches and at 07:30 hours two of these drew alongside the dinghies and took off the survivors.

There was, however, more to come. The RN launches were attacked by two Focke Wulf 190 fighters and hit one of them in return fire. A Condor and a Ju 88 were 'drawn off' by Beaufighters. At 17:20 hours the launches entered Newlyn Harbour in Cornwall with the survivors who had by then been at sea for 124 hours.

A rescue which was completed but which could have gone better, took place in May 1943 and emphasised the need at the time for the better training of crews in emergency procedures and the justification for the establishment of the Air Sea Rescue School at Blackpool which had in fact opened its doors only a fortnight earlier.

A Lancaster was hit by flak crossing the

Mark I Anson *(Bruce Robertson)*.

Dutch coast and had to ditch. After spinning down to 8,000 ft the captain jettisoned some remaining bombs and gave a ditching order to his crew at 4,000 ft (An official report said that he should have done this much sooner so that the wireless operator could have begun sending distress calls from a higher altitude. In fact by the time the wireless operator got his signal off the aircraft was too low for a fix to be obtained from ground stations.)

The ditching was successful and the dinghy released. The crew took their emergency packs, wireless transmitter and pigeon container into the dinghy but cut two lines which they thought were holding them on to the sinking aircraft. In fact this action cut adrift some emergency packs containing the signal pistol, a vital part of the dinghy wireless and some other equipment.

One of the pigeons drowned because the container lids had not been closed by the mid-upper gunner whose job it was to do this on ditching. The other pigeon was wet but it was released with a message. It did not reach base.

Twenty-four hours later two Bostons and two Spitfires flew overhead but the crew could not attract their attention because of the missing signal pistol. The wireless would not work because of the missing part. They drifted towards England for four days, hanging a shirt on to their dinghy mast and early on the fifth day they were taken aboard a minesweeper eight miles off Dungeness.

'Their 129 hours in the dinghy might have been considerably reduced had they known the correct distress procedure, their knowledge of which had never been checked since their arrival at their parent Station', was the laconic comment in an official report.

The rescue of the crew of a Whitley from the Operational Training Unit at St Eval in June 1943 demonstrated lessons which were to hold good for many years. They were carrying out their second anti-submarine patrol in the Western Approaches south-west of Cornwall when their starboard engine failed. They ditched reasonably successfully but heavily, and their SOS message was relayed by a Halifax flying in the vicinity. The crew, all suffering minor injuries, boarded the dinghy in the approved manner.

In the general excitement, however, the kite needed to extend the emergency wireless aerial was left behind. Again in the haste of cutting adrift from a sinking aeroplane an emergency pack was lost, but at least the dinghy wireless left floating in the water was retrieved.

The aircraft sank in six minutes. The Captain decided that although their 'Q' type dinghy had sails it would be better for them to stay in the position he had given on ditching to assist search aircraft. He therefore ordered the laying-out of the drogue sea-anchor and decided to ration himself and his crew to NO food or water for at least two days.

Shore-based rescue services worked out a position of 48°N 15°W from the SOS and all aircraft in the area were advised of this approximate position.

A Whitley was sighted on the afternoon of the first day and the ditched crew tried to make the dinghy wireless work by holding the aerial high in their hands — having lost the kite in the initial ditching. That did not work so the crew tucked themselves in for the night as best they could under the weather aprons. The next morning they decided to hoist sails and steer for home. None of them had any sailing experience but instruction books and diagrams in the survival kit were read carefully and after some difficulties the 'Q' dinghy became a sailing vessel and a course was set for the Scillies.

Two aircraft, one carrying an airborne lifeboat, were despatched by 279 Air Sea Rescue Squadron but found nothing in the bad weather. (The official record does not state whether these were Hudsons or Warwicks — more probably the latter.) A Sunderland spotted the dinghy sail, however — proving yet another argument in favour of fitting survival dinghies with sails.

The Sunderland captain made an attempt to alight along the swell but took off again, then tried an approach into the swell. In attempting this he stalled and dived into the sea with his wingtip floats carried away. The Sunderland crew were able to board their own 'J' type dinghy apart from the Captain who was lost. The Sunderland sank in sixteen minutes, the fourth aircraft of its type to be lost in a rescue attempt involving alighting on an ocean swell.

The Whitley crew then sailed their dinghy across to join up with the Sunderland survivors, tying both boats together, furling sail and streaming a sea anchor again.

A destroyer and several aircraft searched for them all through the night and the next

Protective armament on an RAF Launch *(RAF)*.

day and at dusk they were sighted at position 47°50′N 9°34′W. Early next morning Sunderland 'E' of 461 Squadron spotted one of their red Very lights. This time the Sunderland alighted successfully and took the two groups of survivors aboard. Two hours later the destroyer reached the scene and they were transferred, the Sunderland captain (like many others before and after him) having found the sea to be much rougher than it had looked from the air and having temporarily abandoned the idea of taking off again.

The destroyer took the flying boat in tow and after 3½ hours its Captain decided to take off with a reduced crew. During the take-off both wingtip floats were carried away but its

Aircrew exercising in one-man dinghies with RAF pinnaces *(RAF)*.

An RAF launch in heavy weather (RAF). Note — this and the picture below were taken post-war but illustrate the sort of sea conditions in which RAF High Speed Launches, Pinnaces and other craft operated during wartime rescue operations. There was seldom anyone around with the time or the camera position to take such pictures during actual operations.

resourceful Captain made a successful *landing* on grass at Angle aerodrome in Pembrokeshire with little damage, thus proving something about the strengths and weaknesses of Sunderlands.

Although it only involved a search aircraft in the last stages, the survival story of the ten-man crew of a USAAF Fortress taking part in a daylight raid on Hamburg on 25 July 1943 deserves recording for posterity to demonstrate the tenacity and courage of all concerned and the ruggedness of the aircraft type.

The aircraft was straddled by intense flak and attacked by swarms of German fighters both before and after bombing its target. By the time the Fortress had crossed the coast on its way home three engines had been hit, the port wing extensively damaged and the Navigator and Bombardier blown back out of their nose positions by exploding 20 mm shells — miraculously without serious injury.

As the Captain prepared to ditch fighters continued to attack and at one stage he was forced to put his aircraft into a steep dive just as the bruised and battered Bombardier was trying to assemble the rest of the crew in the radio room. The sudden dive threw the

The crew of a Halifax about to be picked up by an RAF launch *(IWM)*.

Walrus picking up survivor. Probably a training or demonstration picture to judge from the relaxed expressions! *(RAF)*.

Two of the few pictures taken of a 'live' rescue. An aircrew being brought aboard No *149*. Note scrambling net and defensive armament *(RAF)*.

Bombardier nearly out of the top hatch which had been opened preparatory to ditching but he managed to hang on to the edge of it until he was thrown back in again as his Captain levelled out.

Meanwhile the waist and tail gunner, believing the aircraft to be shot down out of control, disregarded their chances of parachuting and went on firing at the enemy fighters. The fighters pressed home their attacks until the moment of ditching, which the Fortress Captain carried out with total coolness, making a slow glide in with full flaps down but with only one engine running.

The sea was smooth and although the dinghies had to be pulled out of the wing housings by the ball turret gunner and one had been punctured earlier by flak, the crew managed to pump them up, board them and patch them. They tied the two dinghies together, took stock of their rations and water and planned their use so that they would last for ten days.

After 38 hours in the dinghies they sighted a small sailing boat and paddled towards it. About three hours later the boat picked them up. The official report does not disclose the nationality of this vessel — perhaps for security reasons at the time — but it was probably either Dutch or Danish. The boat's skipper told the aircrew that he had at first hesitated about picking them up because he thought they were Germans

The aircrew noticed that the boat was sailing east and they indicated that they would sooner re-board their dinghies, perhaps with supplies of fresh water and food rather than stay aboard on that course. The sailing boat skipper then agreed to take them to within fifty miles of the English coast.

The next morning a Halifax circled over them and the aircrew painted in white letters on a piece of dark tarpaulin the words: 'SOS Bring Boat'. They also waved their life jackets. The Halifax signalled by Aldis lamp: 'Rescue Launch Coming'. Two hours later an RAF Air Sea Rescue launch arrived.

The boat skipper was given supplies of petrol, food and tobacco and he turned away for his home port, wherever it was. Nobody quite knew.

Chapter 3
Rescues by airborne lifeboats

The Airborne Lifeboat was one of the most successful, yet least publicly recognised devices for the saving of life during World War 2. Its lack of recognition may have had something to do with wartime security in that airborne lifeboat rescues were seldom publicised and indeed all concerned with them were instructed that the boats must be sunk without trace unless they could be towed back safely into a friendly port. Most details of airborne lifeboat rescues were only released some years after the conclusion of World War 2.

It has been difficult to establish exactly how many lives were saved by this invention — which, as earlier stated, should really be credited to Group Captain (later Air Commodore) Waring, RAF, and Lieutenant Robb, RNVR, with Mr Uffa Fox as the 'perfector' — but a fellow author, Mr Stephen Daniels, who is preparing a specialist book on the subject has estimated that at least 65 operational drops were carried out.

Airborne Lifeboat (probably Mark II) being fitted to a Warwick *(Bruce Robertson)*.

In addition to the boats carried by the Hudsons and Warwicks of the home-based air-sea rescue squadrons others were deployed in the Middle and Far East and some were carried and dropped by USAAF aircraft.

A fundamental idea behind the evolution of the Airborne Lifeboat was that it could be a means of rescue for airmen finding themselves in the water close to enemy coasts with the necessity to get themselves away from the scene as quickly as possible. Because of their shallow draught they were often sailed successfully through minefields to safer waters where larger craft could rendezvous with them.

Three types were produced and used during much of the war. These were the Mark 1, fitted to the Hudsons of the first batch of ASR squadrons, the Mark 1A rapidly evolved to fit into the Warwicks which were brought into service to replace the ageing Hudsons, and the Mark 2, which was an improved version fitted to Warwicks and other aircraft types. A Mark 3 boat was on the stocks towards the end of the war and became the equipment for several ASR squadrons in the immediate post-war years. They were carried by ASR 3 Lancasters which formed an important component of Coastal Command, by some prototype Shackletons, and by some of the first batch of the latter type aircraft purchased by South Africa in 1957.

The Mark 1 and 1A boats were made of mahogany, weighed 1,500 lb fully equipped, had a buoyancy of 3,400 lb, were 23-ft 6 in long with a beam of 5 ft 6 in. They 'drew' about 10 in of water and were initially fitted with twin 'Middy' outboard/inboard petrol engines. Theoretically one engine could give them a range of 110 nautical miles at 4 1/2 knots and two engines could give them 65 nm

A Mark III Airborne Lifeboat being loaded into an ASR III Lancaster, probably in Malta *circa* 1950
(IWM).

at seven knots. These boats had a maximum carrying capacity of sixteen survivors but in most operations a maximum of ten (the average Fortress crew) boarded them. A mainsail of 75 sq ft was provided and a foresail of 34 sq ft, plus four long oars.

Survival equipment loaded aboard included a T 1333 wireless, a Very pistol and cartridges, a torch, an Aldis signal lamp, fourteen 'Everhot' bags, first aid kit, cans of fresh water, food, cigarettes, matches and waterproof clothing.

One of the last Airborne Lifeboats in preservation. This is a SARO Mark III, one of several fitted to the first batch of Shackletons supplied to the South African Air Force in 1957. This boat is preserved in the SAAF Museum, Pretoria. Another ABL is preserved at the RAF Museum, Hendon, and it is believed that a few, converted into yachts of a sort, may lie around on creeks in the British Isles
(Louis Vosloo).

A Saunders Roe Mark III Airborne Lifeboat fitted to a South African Air Force Mark III Shackleton
(British Aerospace/Avro).

Mark 1 and 1A boats were not only carried and dropped from Hudsons and Warwicks but also from Fortresses operated both by the RAF and by the USAAF, and by a small number of Fleet Air Arm Barracudas. The Mark 2 boats were 30-ft long overall, weighed 3,000 lb and most were fitted with Austin 12 hp marine engines. The Mark 3s were made of light alloy, were 32-ft long and weighed 4,400 lb. They carried 117 sq ft mainsails and 52 sq ft foresails. Most were fitted with Vincent HRD two-stroke horizontally-opposed engines capable of developing nearly 14 hp.

In all cases the boats had to be carefully shaped so that the lines of their gunwales conformed with those of the underside of the carrier aircraft and with their own undersides giving adequate ground clearance during taxying or tail-down landings.

Records available indicate that the minds of Group Captain Waring, Lieutenant Robb and Uffa Fox were working on parallel lines.

In his own book *Joys of Life* (published by Newnes in 1966) Uffa Fox recorded that at an early stage of the war he had been called on to design protective clothing, sails and paddles which would enable downed airmen to live longer. This work, he said, convinced him of the urgent need of saving their lives and legs by taking their rescue to a stage that would bring them safely home.

In his book he recorded that knowing the Hudsons were in use for air-sea rescue he set to work to design a folding boat which would go inside this aircraft's bomb bay. He described how his idea for this folding boat was modelled on the tea table at his Isle of Wight home with thick drawing paper and strawberry jam. The idea of a folding boat to be stowed inside the bomb bay of a Hudson did not work because of the internal dimensions so Uffa Fox and his colleagues, he recalled, went on to design and develop the first true airborne lifeboat.

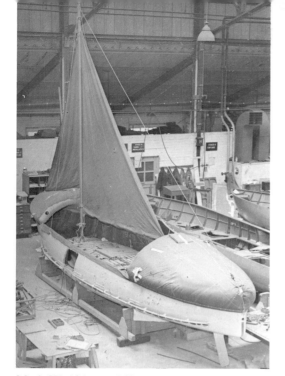

Mark III Airborne Lifeboats under construction and on test at the then Saunders Roe factory, Beaumaris, Anglesey *(Laird, Anglesey, Ltd)*.

In his book he described in detail how his skilled craftsmen evolved a boat of the right dimensions and construction within a few days of non-stop work and how it was quickly proved to be successful. Argument may, of course, go on as to who was the true inventor and designer of the Airborne Lifeboat — Group Captain Waring or Uffa Fox. In any case it turned out to be a magnificent piece of work, probably of joint work with the name of the obscure Lieutenant Robb, RNVR, most certainly deserving of association. In the immediate post-war years one of the first sailing schools to be established to cater for a growing demand — the Plymouth Sailing School — purchased some war-surplus Airborne Lifeboats and used them successfully for many years. Group Captain, later Air Commodore, Waring, died in 1987.

The hull shapes as finally evolved by Uffa Fox bore resemblance to those of some of his many successful racing yachts but one feature was a marked 'tumblehome' with maximum width on the waterline to give stability and a gradual taper upwards and inwards to bring the distance across the beam between the gunwales within the limits prescribed by the dimensions of the carrier aircraft fuselage.

They were built with 'turtlebacks' at bow and stern to assist self-righting — making them look rather like the earlier generations of RNLI lifeboats. These, of course, had to be inflatable so that the hull top was flat when in position on the aircraft. As well as the turtlebacks there were other buoyancy chambers automatically inflated by CO_2 gas when the boat was dropped.

In addition to the survival equipment the boats carried sealed instruction booklets on both sailing principles and engine starting procedures. It is intriguing to note that the sailing instructions in the Airborne Lifeboats and in some rescue dinghies fitted with sails bear a marked resemblance to the manuals still used at Royal Yachting Association approved sailing schools.

Details of many of the rescue operations indicate that survivors often had difficulty starting the engines and keeping them running at full power. This is perhaps not surprising since these were the days before sealed ignition systems and that remarkable fluid called WD 40. Petrol engines of the 1940s never took kindly to drenching by salt water and this was often unavoidable.

Aircrew training with Mark I Airborne Lifeboats in 1944 at Fleetwood *(Reg Thackeray)*.

A ditched Fortress, its crew in two life rafts, and an Airborne Lifeboat descending on three parachutes. Note trail of smoke flare indicating wind direction and the obviously skilful ditching which has been carried out by the Fortress pilots *(RAF)*.

The standard dropping procedure was to release the boat at between 600 and 700 ft altitude while flying into wind at about 120 mph. The boats were supported during drop either by six small parachutes, sometimes three larger ones. As the falling boat took on a nose-down attitude balance switches triggered off the CO_2 bottles to inflate the buoyancy compartments and others fired a series of rockets, one to launch a drogue sea anchor to hold the bows into wind, others to project 150-ft long floating ropes either side to help survivors make contact and climb aboard.

Mark IX bombsights were used to judge the precise moment for release and in a perfectly judged/drop survivors in a dinghy would drift down on the lifeboat which was held almost stationary by its drogue.

Opportunities for practice drills were limited and there was often some trepidation among the ASR aircrews when carrying out their first operational drops. Mr John Sumner, a Warrant Officer navigator of the Royal Australian Air Force serving with 278

ASR Squadron recalls finding the crew of a USAAF Liberator in the sea off the Dutch/Belgian coast on 20 July 1944.

Coastal Command and the USAAF had already flown nearly eighty sorties in search of the crew and at the end of a creeping line-ahead search pattern the rear gunner of Sumner's Warwick *(BV478)* said he thought he had seen a faint and distant red light. By the use of 'Gee' fixes and the bearing of the light John Sumner brought his pilot (Warrant Officer Mike McVeigh, Royal New Zealand Air Force) over the top of two dinghies containing the nine crew members of the Liberator.

The sea was rough and although it was daylight visibility was poor with solid cloud down to 1,000 ft. 'This was my first and only drop, in fact I believe it was our squadron's first; so with fingers crossed I pressed the release. Everything worked perfectly and within minutes the survivors were aboard and tucking into cans of self-heating soup.

'Unfortunately the boat must have suffered some damage as the crew had no luck in starting the engine and we called up the High Speed Launches from Dover. As we were only eight miles north-west of Ostend and flying lazy circles at 300 ft we were very relieved when two hours later the launches came charging over the horizon to complete the job.

'So that they could make a quick exit they rammed and sank our lifeboat, a sad sight that we were spared as by then we were dashing home on near empty tanks.'

The first six operational Airborne Lifeboat drops were recorded in some detail and the reports circulated as training aids by the Directorate of Aircraft Safety. The first was carried out on 5 May 1943 when Halifax 'V' of No 102 Squadron ditched fifty miles east of Spurn Point after being hit by flak over its Dortmund target, resulting in the loss of two engines. The aircraft crossed the Dutch coast at 8,000 ft, gradually losing height. It was a moonless night with a light north-easterly wind.

The ditching was carried out skilfully across the swell with thirty degrees of flap down. The crew all got clear but the aircraft dinghy did not release itself, and as on many other occasions it had to be pulled out of its stowage manually — in this case by the Captain of the aircraft. However, it did inflate properly. The emergency packs were brought aboard but again, as on many other

occasions, the emergency radio was left behind.

For three hours no rescue or search aircraft were sighted but at 06:25 hours an ASR Hudson was seen, Very lights were fired, and the rescue aircraft fixed and radioed the dinghy position as 53°40′N 01°26′E. Just over an hour later another ASR Hudson ('W') carrying a lifeboat was overhead followed quickly by Hudson ('Y'). The Hudsons first dropped smoke floats and then 'W' dropped its lifeboat.

One report of this event, published in the semi-secret *Coastal Command Review* of the year said: 'The crew of the Hudson hardly dared breathe as the Airborne Lifeboat went down, for this was the first time it had been used operationally.

'To their delight the parachutes blossomed out beautifully and the boat floated gently down, slightly nose first, and settled on the water no more than 20 yd downwind of the dinghy.'

The *Coastal Command Review* report of the incident went on to say: 'The bomber crew at first thought that the bottom of the Hudson had fallen off. To their amazement and joy, after they had recovered from their initial fright, they realised that it was a *boat* floating down on three parachutes.

'The lifeboat landed on the water with a

Rescuers sometimes got into trouble themselves. The original caption to this picture of Warwick *BV475* of 278 Squadron after arrival at Bradwell Bay with imminent engine failure was: 'Has anyone seen our lifeboat!' *(John Sumner)*.

splash. The parachutes floated away having been automatically released directly the boat touched water. The dinghy crew soon paddled to the lifeboat and climbed aboard. After a preliminary investigation two engines, a large compass and a rudder were found. While one member of the crew, who was the engineer, started the engine another fixed the rudder in its place.

'In a few minutes the airmen/sailors were under way at a steady six knots. The Hudson then flashed by Aldis lamp a course to steer. From then until they were intercepted by, and taken aboard, an Air Sea Rescue High Speed Launch approximately fourteen miles from shore air cover was provided by ASR aircraft based in the area.'

A slightly different view of this operation was published in 'Air Sea Rescue Note No 66' issued on 10 June 1943. This report said that the Halifax crew had never heard of Airborne Lifeboats and were curious about the peculiarly shaped Hudson flying above them. 'Their astonishment was great when "the bottom of the Hudson fell off" and they saw that it was a boat, even noting that it had propellers protruding from the bottom.'

The ASR Note disclosed that the sea anchor drogue rocket had failed to fire and that the self-righting buoyancy chambers had failed to inflate. Another thing which had gone wrong was that the parachute slings had been fitted the wrong way round so that the boat hit the water in much too flat an attitude resulting in some leaking and flooding of the engine compartments. The line-throwing rockets also failed on this, the very first operation. (The official reports on this incident and those on others to follow show clearly that operational experience was needed before the Airborne Lifeboat techniques could be perfected.)

In spite of a lot of the refinements having gone wrong the Halifax crew boarded the lifeboat ('with ease' according to the ASR Note) although two of them were injured and the rest were wet, cramped and seasick after five hours in their dinghy. The Halifax engineer and the navigator (who had some yachting experience) started the two engines and 'noted the smoothness of their running'. The captain shipped the rudder and the wireless operator read an Aldis lamp signal

from an aircraft above telling them to steer on a course of 214 degrees magnetic. Quite soon they were on this course at a steady six knots with their own dinghy still in tow.

The dinghy broke its painter and was sunk by gunfire from an escorting Hudson. (It was, in 1943, and still is, in 1987, important for abandoned rescue dinghies to be sunk by some means to prevent false alarms.) Shortly before noon low cloud separated the escorting aircraft from sight of the lifeboat and one of the engines failed because of a fractured propeller shear pin. The Halifax crew then rigged the mast and the mainsail.

At 13:00 hours a Hudson search aircraft spotted the lifeboat again, making slow progress with fog developing. The crew wrote the message 'Engine US' with fluorescine dye on the sail.

Royal Air Force High Speed Launch No 2579 and two Royal Navy RMLs (Rescue Motor Launches) were given a new position and with some guidance from an Anson and a Walrus, HSL 2579 closed in, took the Halifax crew aboard and landed them at Grimsby where they were admitted to the Royal Navy sick quarters for 48 hours.

Mr Cyril Shutt, who was the Coxswain of HSL 2579 recalls being sent out for a square search from Grimsby that day. He and his launch crew were given a position of about ten miles East of the Dudgeon Buoy and remembers a wireless signal saying: 'Power dinghy dropped in position . . .'

In 1985 Mr Shutt said: 'We'd never heard of an airborne lifeboat, but we knew of a power dinghy which was a nine-foot boat fitted with a Ford engine for ferrying airmen and mechanics out to moored flying boats. We said "What the Hell's a power dinghy doing out there?"

'So we proceeded to the position where it was supposed to have been dropped. The message didn't say who'd dropped it. We presumed it was some aircraft, thinking it was one from an Operational Training Unit — they used to do patrol jobs and searches as part of their training.

'Anyway we got to this position and in the distance saw some blue sails and we said: "What the Hell's that?" At that time there were a lot of Danes and Norwegians escaping and thought perhaps it was one of them.

'It turned out to be an Airborne Lifeboat. Apparently they couldn't start the engine but they had bags of rations aboard. One of them had a bit of sailing experience and they were sailing home. I remember the sea was slight to moderate at that time, just an occasional popple, about Force 4. We went alongside, got their wet clothing off, got them into dry clothing and got this thing in tow. It was a hell of a job, sheering to port and starboard, but we eventually managed to get it all right.

'There's one more point. We were in a minefield, because when we came back we made the airborne lifeboat fast to a swept channel buoy — one of those marked when the sweepers had been through, about 25 miles south-east of Grimsby. We sent a message through to tell them what we'd done and that we were going back to Grimsby with the survivors. About ten hours later a Naval patrol boat brought the lifeboat in.'

Several of the failings of this, the first Airborne Lifeboat in operational use, were rectified immediately afterwards and many important lessons were learned by all concerned. Other steps were eventually taken to 'educate' aircrews on what an airborne lifeboat looked like — several accounts reveal that survivors were somewhat astonished when one descended upon them.

The second operational drop was to the crew of a Wellington which had been 'nickelling' (dropping leaflets) over France in July 1943. They were hit by flak causing failure of the port engine and a ditching was carried out in bright moonlight and into six-foot waves about seven miles off the French coast. The flap controls had been put out of action so the captain had to put the aircraft down at about 85 mph and it was quickly flooded, sinking in fifteen minutes.

The six crew members, some of them bruised and exhausted, got clear with some difficulty and boarded their dinghy shortly after two o'clock in the morning. They drifted ESE until the French coast appeared at about half past eight. They then began paddling. Again because of the rapid flooding of the aircraft they had been unable to get the emergency wireless transmitter aboard.

Just after midday some Typhoons sighted them fifteen miles west of Le Havre, trying to make to the north against a tidal stream. They

kept paddling all that day and through the night and the following morning they were again sighted by Typhoons eight miles off Cap d'Antifer.

In spite of all their efforts they were still getting dangerously close to the French coast when a Hudson of 279 ASR Squadron carrying a lifeboat appeared. The crew trailed fluorescine and fired Very lights. Again there were some malfunctions when the boat was dropped. The drogue rocket failed to fire but the boat struck the water nose down with only a 'a little splash'. The self-righting chambers failed to inflate and the line throwing rockets did not fire. The stern canvas cover was split, the mainsail sheet carried away and the boat finished up twenty yards upwind of the dinghy. Nevertheless the crew were able to paddle to the lifeboat and board it. They tried to sink their dinghy with a knife, failed, and so cut it adrift in the hope that it would act as a decoy for the enemy.

With the Captain reading out the instruction booklet — having to shout at the top of his voice above the noise of escorting aircraft — the rest of the crew set about starting the engines, rigging the rudder and centreboard and blowing up the buoyancy chambers with a hand pump. Within twenty minutes of the drop they had set a course of due north magnetic. One engine stopped temporarily but they re-started it in five minutes. They decided to motor to mid-Channel and then set sail. After they had covered thirty miles at a healthy average speed of 7 1/2 knots they were met by High Speed Launches Nos *177* and *190* some 37 miles NW of Cap d'Antifer.

The crew took care to tidy the boat and make it look shipshape before the 'professional seamen' came alongside. They then boarded HSL *177* while No *190* towed the lifeboat to base, having started to disable it and prepare it for sinking on an order from shore which was later rescinded. The Wellington crew, who had obviously rather taken to the nautical life, claimed that if they had not been met by the launches they would have sailed into the Solent by nightfall.

A comment on this rescue by the Directorate of Aircraft Safety said that lifeboats which had served their purpose should be sunk rather than prejudice the

This sequence of photographs shows an
Airborne Lifeboat being dropped to the
American crew of a Catalina on 3 April 1945.
The Catalina had been searching for the pilot of
a fighter which had been forced down and then
got in trouble itself, having to alight in heavy
seas resulting in the crew taking to their dinghy
and being adrift for five days before being
sighted by a Warwick, which dropped the
lifeboat. The first picture shows the lifeboat
descending on six parachutes. Just discernible
above them is another small parachute carrying
survival equipment. The second picture shows
the lifeboat nearly upright with one buoyancy
compartment inflated and the parachutes in
process of being automatically cut away. The
third picture shows the Catalina crew aboard
the lifeboat with both buoyancy compartments
inflated *(IWM)*.

safety of surface vessels or aircraft but that if
salvage was possible — particularly after
malfunctions — valuable lessons could be
learned, which they presumably were in this
case.

The third drop, a 'copybook' operation,
occurred on 26 July 1943 when a Fortress
with a crew of ten ditched off Cromer. One of
the aircraft dinghies inflated satisfactorily but
the other leaked badly with two crew
members aboard it and two in the water
hanging on to it. They were sighted soon after
the ditching by an ASR aircraft carrying a
lifeboat — the Fortress was still floating.

The sea was slight and there was a light
south-westerly wind. The lifeboat-carrying
aircraft approached at 105 mph and the drop

was made from 700 ft, alighting well clear of the dinghies and of an oil slick on the water. The parachutes deployed correctly, the drogue rocket fired, both self-righting compartments inflated and the boat descended without any swing.

'The dinghy crews had not heard of the Airborne Lifeboat and were duly impressed' said the official report later.

The floating rope rockets also fired correctly and after paddling about eighty yards the survivors in the undamaged dinghy were able to grasp the port side ropes and draw themselves alongside. The six men in the lifeboat then rigged the oars and rowed to their comrades in and clinging to the punctured dinghy which was cut adrift to be sunk by gunfire from escorting aircraft.

The survivors had difficulty starting the engines and the instruction book was illegible. However, they hoisted sail and got under way on a course of 220 degrees about an hour after their ditching. They used the emergency wireless from the undamaged dinghy which they were still towing to transmit a position, flying the aerial by its kite. They put on the waterproof jackets provided, smoked the cigarettes and ate the chocolate. They sailed twenty miles in just under five hours and were met by High Speed Launch 2551 which brought them all ashore.

Another Fortress crew from No 460 Squadron, USAAF figured in the fourth drop which took place later the same day. Their aircraft, a B-17 No F230206, actually ditched on 25 July after having been attacked by three Fw 190s over the Danish coast. Two dinghies were released and were tied together with all but one crew member safely aboard, together with full survival kit and a wireless set.

They drifted for nineteen hours and during the night were able to see and hear the bombing of Hamburg. They transmitted wireless signals at half-hourly intervals in daylight hours only and began paddling west on the morning of 26 July. Just after midday they saw two Lancasters apparently searching, whose attention was attracted by the firing of signal flares. The Lancasters then dropped three sets of Lindholme Gear and the survivors were able to board the big dinghies, making use of the many comforts stowed in them. They tied all three dinghies together.

Hudsons, one carrying an Airborne Lifeboat, were overhead at 20:10 hours and a drop with all systems functioning was made almost immediately. The survivors boarded the lifeboat and escort aircraft sank all the dinghies. The survivors in the lifeboat had some difficulties with the engines but after about 45 minutes had them both running well at half-throttle. They stepped the mast and rigged the sails but did not use them while the engines were running.

During the night heavy following seas caused damage to the tiller attachments but the crew managed to rig steering lines, rather like those used by ladies steering rowing skiffs on the Serpentine and elsewhere. Early the next morning a Danish sailing smack was sighted with four men aboard. Friendly waves were exchanged, the aircrew plus their lifeboat were hauled aboard and the Skipper of the smack set course for England.

More ASR aircraft appeared overhead and in the early evening RAF High Speed Launches Nos 2551 and 184 came alongside. After consumption of a bottle of rum the Danes agreed to sail to England, all arriving at Yarmouth just before midnight.

An inspection of the salvaged lifeboat showed that it was totally undamaged in the drop and that all the rocket gear had functioned correctly. A few more lessons were learned, however, about rigging, particularly about the assembly of the rudder and tiller, all of which were promulgated throughout the RAF and the USAAF.

Drop number five again involved a Fortress, No 42/3035 which had been attacked by Fw 190s over Kiel on 28 July. Three engines were damaged and the aircraft, escorted by another Fortress damaged with one engine out, lost height over the sea with its starboard wing beginning to catch fire. The Fortress Captain put his aeroplane into a dive, without using flap so as not to strain the burning wing any further. The crew jettisoned everything they could lay hands on and throw out.

On ditching the tail broke off and five crew members were lost, presumably drowned. The pilot (Captain) and the Engineer carried out some very gallant work, getting a dinghy out of its housing manually. The Engineer, who had first left the sinking aircraft via the

Some typical Warwick ASR six-man aircrews.
The Captains are Len Harvey and Jim Forrest
(Jim Forrest).

radio hatch, went back inside to pull the dinghy releases. The pilot dragged the dinghy out from on top of the wing but was himself sucked down several feet before it inflated. All the survival equipment packed into the aircraft was lost.

The five remaining survivors got into the dinghy without difficulty, took off their heavy clothing and boots and threw them overboard. The accompanying Fortress continued circling at 500 ft until the ditched crew survivors were seen to be safely aboard the dinghy and then climbed away.

The aircraft had ditched at about 09:45 and between 15:00 and 16:00 hours the survivors saw three search aircraft and fired flares without apparent effect. They streamed their fluorescine markers, fired one more flare and were seen. The search aircraft circled them and at about 17:45 hours two Hudsons of 279

ASR Squadron appeared, one carrying a lifeboat.

The drop was successful, the boat landing gently about 100 ft away from them. They boarded, read the instructions and started both engines. The port engine gave trouble during the night but they had both running well the next morning and travelled 100 miles until picked up by a High Speed Launch at about 22:00 hours.

The crew of Mitchell 'Q' of 226 Squadron who were eventually rescued in Operational Airborne Lifeboat Drop number six after ditching on 30 July 1943 had a much rougher time. Their aircraft was itself engaged in an air-sea rescue search in the North Sea and had been circling a dinghy for three hours when they were bounced by eight enemy fighters.

With both engines on fire they had to ditch with the aircraft sinking immediately. Only the observer, wireless operator and air gunner escaped into a dinghy. They found three other single-seat dinghies in the water, inflated them and made them fast alongside. They soon saw two Hudsons and several enemy aircraft overhead. They cut the aprons off the single-seat 'K' dinghies and used them for cover in the bigger one they had boarded. In the evening Beaufighters circled them and signalled that help was coming.

The next day (31 July) four Beaufighters with two Hudsons appeared. One of the latter, 'R' of 279 Squadron, carried a lifeboat. The survivors later reported that the lifeboat-carrying Hudson's pilot was 'most careful' in dropping the boat. He dropped a smoke float first and made several runs into wind at 700 ft before making the drop.

The bow of the boat seemed to drop first (as it should have done) and three parachutes deployed simultaneously. The drogue rocket fired and the self-righting chambers inflated as the boat alighted exactly where it should have done 100 yd to one side of, and slightly downwind of the dinghy. The parachutes collapsed, were automatically released and blew clear, and the line-throwing rockets fired. In short another 'copybook' drop.

The three survivors then cut the 'K' dinghies adrift and paddled their main 'A2' to the lifeboat which they boarded without difficulty. They destroyed the large dinghy themselves and the escorting Beaufighters sank the small ones. One of the Beaufighters signalled to them by Aldis lamp to steer on 247 degrees, just south of west.

The survivors found both engine lockers dry but had some trouble fitting the rudder. They stepped the mast, set the mainsail and steered the prescribed course with both engines eventually running at half throttle. Then things started to go wrong. The southeast wind increased and waves built up. As it grew dark both engines stopped, apparently 'drowned'. They pumped out the engine compartments, lowered the mainsail and tried to sail under jib only. The tiller arm then broke and the boat broached across the seas which poured inboard.

A rough and nasty night followed with the mast and foresail lowered, the latter lashed on to the drogue in an effort to make a big enough sea anchor to hold them into wind and wave. On the night of Sunday 1 August waves continued to wash over them. At dawn the improvised sea anchor carried away and they were left helpless with no rudder, no engine, and no mast.

They changed into the 'waterproof' suits but found they leaked. Their little boat was, however, still rising well to the cross waves and they managed to correct a list to starboard by pumping out some compartments and letting water into others. They pumped and baled continuously for six hours on the Sunday. On the afternoon of that day three Hudsons sighted them, circled them and left. Then three Bostons did the same thing. They settled down to another, marginally more comfortable, night.

On the Monday (August Bank Holiday for others) they made more valiant efforts to start the engines without success. They rigged an oar as a mast and set the foresail, but the wind had turned SW, creating much leeway in the wrong direction. They were becoming tired and took turns to sleep under the bow self-righting compartment. They rationed themselves to a daily issue of one tin of water, one tin of milk and nine Horlicks tablets each. None were seasick.

At 07:30 they sighted three Mitchells to the south and fired flares without success. At 14:00 and 15:00 they were seen by single Mitchells, each of which subsequently lost sight of them. At 18:00 they were sighted by a Halifax which stayed over them for several hours. At 19:00 two Hudsons 'joined the circuit', remaining until darkness and signalling to them that help was coming. At 08:00 hours the following morning three more Mitchells sighted them and remained overhead for two hours until relieved by a Hudson and another Mitchell.

At 14:45 hours on 2 August 1943 two Royal Navy rescue launches closed up with them, took them aboard and towed their faithful lifeboat back to base, which was reached on the evening of Wednesday 3 August.

Many more successful rescues by Airborne Lifeboats were conducted in World War 2. Here follow details of some of those in which records were kept and have been made available.

On 7 January 1944 a Mosquito of 157 Squadron, 19 Group, ditched in the Bay of Biscay after it and others had tangled with two Ju 88s, one of which was shot down. During the fight both engines of Mosquito '11 E' were hit and stopped. Since he was down to 3,000 ft about 170 miles SW of Land's End the pilot appreciated that there was no point in trying to send a distress signal direct to base so he told his fellow pilots over the short range RT that he was ditching and then proceeded so to do.

The weather conditions were fair with a long heavy SW swell and choppy cross seas. The pilot carried out a classic ditching parallel to the swell with tail down and full flaps on. There were two impacts and the aircraft came to rest with the tail unit broken off. The navigator and pilot both got clear in less than a minute. The pilot had his 'K' one-man dinghy with him but the navigator forgot his in the excitement; nevertheless they also had a two-man 'L' type dinghy to share if necessary.

They found themselves in choppy seas and a long heavy swell. The pilot (Captain of the aircraft) decided to let his navigator, who was described as being 'above average in stature and physique', use the 'L' dinghy while he occupied the smaller 'K' type. They tied themselves together and settled down for a cold, wet and windy night. At dawn they hoisted the sail in the 'K' dinghy and got under way on a north-easterly course, still towing the 'L' dinghy and achieving about one knot of speed.

At noon the following day they were overjoyed to see four Mosquitoes of their own squadron circling them, and soon afterwards five Beaufighters. These sights stimulated their slightly flagging spirits and they became confident of rescue. At about 13:00 hours Warwick 'E' of 280 ASR Squadron dropped an Airborne Lifeboat 100 yd downwind of them. They manoeuvred their dinghies alongside separately, the navigator in some style using his dinghy apron as a sail. They took the 'K' dinghy on board the lifeboat and abandoned the other. Inside the lifeboat they found a message saying: 'Steer 350 degrees True or 003 Magnetic. Good Luck'.

They could not at first start the engines but the Mosquito Captain saw that the lifeboat parachutes had not blown clear and that some of their lines were fouling the propeller. He stripped off, dived over the side and cut the lines clear. The starboard engine then started and the recommended course was set at about three knots. This engine stopped after a while and it was found that its propeller had been fouled by a wire from the drogue rocket. However, they then started the port engine. No aircraft nor surface craft were seen during the day and they worked out a rationing system which would last them for four weeks if necessary.

At dawn on Sunday 9 January the port engine stopped, partly because they had let the tank run dry before refuelling. They also found both propellers badly fouled and not being able to clear them they stepped the mast and rigged the sails. Although neither had any sailing experience they followed the instruction pamphlet and were able to resume a course of 350 degrees True. By this time they were coping with a strong south-westerly wind, rough seas and a heavy swell with rain showers.

About three hours before dusk a Wellington was sighted on the horizon and they fired red star signals without success. As night fell the wind and sea increased so they hove-to with sails furled and the sea anchor streamed. They saw two Ju 88s about a mile north and estimated their position at nightfall to be about sixty miles SW of Ushant.

In the early hours of Monday 10 January the wind and sea abated so they hoisted sail again, steering on 340 degrees True to allow for the drift which had probably occurred during the night. They estimated they were making between four and five knots. They said afterwards that at this stage they had to fight off an almost overwhelming desire to turn for the French coast but fought it off with a resolution to sail into Mount's Bay, Cornwall.

In the afternoon of the Monday a Mosquito circled them, waggled its wings and flew off to the north. They interpreted this as meaning that their course was too far south so they altered it to 360 degrees True. During the night a large aircraft was heard twice overhead. They fired red star signals without acknowledgment. Later it transpired that this aircraft was a Liberator from St Eval which was searching for them and which to its crew's great credit had spotted a High Speed Launch, also engaged in the search and which was in fact only about seven miles from the lifeboat at the time.

The Liberator made dive runs over the HSL, illuminating it twice by Leigh Light and dropping two flares and a supply of petrol. The HSL in turn tried to establish communications with the Liberator by wireless and lamp without result. It became clear afterwards that in the bad visibility the Liberator had in fact mistaken the HSL for the airborne lifeboat.

At about this time the survivors in the lifeboat altered course to east of north on 040 degrees and held it until dawn of Tuesday 11 January when the wind changed twice. Visibility remained very poor but improved during the night as the wind dropped. During the night engines were heard and two surface craft seen but because the survivors thought the engine noises might be coming from U-boats they took no action. As the vessels came nearer, however, they were recognised as Royal Navy Rescue Motor Launches and the survivors fired a 'Two Star Red' signal. Almost immediately RML No *534* closed on the lifeboat and the occupants jumped aboard in high spirits.

They were put to bed and given expert attention even though they were little the worse for the experiences. Their faithful airborne lifeboat was towed in by RML No *526*. The official report on this rescue said: 'During 103 hours that these two airmen spent afloat they set a very high standard of initiative and skill coupled with great courage, fortitude and determination'.

On 28 January 1944 a Lancaster returning from a Berlin raid on three engines and with other damage had to ditch in the Channel — the crew deciding to adopt this course rather than bale out over France which they could have done. It was pitch dark with a 30 mph wind and a heavy swell.

The ditching in the early hours of the morning was a heavy one. The captain was dragged some 15 ft down into the water before escaping, the tail broke off and three crew members were trapped and drowned. The remaining crew members — captain, navigator, bomb-aimer and wireless operator-managed to board their Mark 3 'J' type dinghy but all the separate survival equipment went down in the aircraft which sank in eight minutes.

At daylight the Guernsey coastline was seen and the survivors began paddling towards it. At 11:00 hours five Spitfires were sighted and the crew's red flares were acknowledged. These and other Spitfires stayed overhead until 13:15 when a Warwick of 280 ASR Squadron dropped an Airborne Lifeboat to them.

The boat initially alighted on its side but righted itself. The rocket-propelled starboard boarding lines landed only 30 ft from the dinghy and the crew boarded without trouble. The boat's engine compartments were badly flooded and neither motor would start. After being given a course of 030 degrees to steer on by Aldis lamp signal from the Warwick the crew decided it would be more prudent to lie to the sea anchor because of the weather conditions. Spitfires stayed overhead and at 17:45 two Motor Torpedo Boats reached them.

The survivors were landed at Dartmouth at 01:00 hours on 29 January. Because of the weather the lifeboat could not be towed in and was sunk by gunfire from a Spitfire.

On 13 June 1944 a Royal Canadian Air Force Catalina (or 'Canso' to be more precise for its particular Mark) captained by Wing Commander Cecil Chapman spotted the Schnorkel mast of U-boat *715* between Norway and Shetland and prepared to attack it. The U-boat's commander, unable to dive in

time, surfaced fully instead to try to fight the aircraft off by gunfire. After being raked with machine-gun fire from the flying boat and straddled with depth charges, the U-boat appeared to sink but then re-surfaced after the gun crew on the conning tower had been flung into the icy cold water.

Somewhat to the astonishment of the Canso crew the gunners swam back to their vessel, manned their weapon again and hit the aircraft, setting one of the engines on fire. Wing Commander Chapman and his co-pilot named McRae had to make a difficult forced landing alighting into heavy seas and together with five of the crew managed to board one leaking dinghy before their badly holed aircraft sank. One crew member was lost but the wireless operator had managed to get off an SOS message with an accurate position. At about the same time the U-boat sank finally, some twenty members of its crew getting clear. The commander shot himself.

Conditions were all against survival for friend and foe alike, cold seas even at that time of the year and strong winds. Two of the flying boat crew were soon seriously affected by exposure.

A Coastal Command Liberator which was in the area circled them and guided in an Airborne Lifeboat-carrying Warwick of 281 ASR Squadron based at Wick. The pilot of the Warwick, David Duthie, now living in Urmston, near Manchester, vividly remembers the scene.

'We could see the U-boat survivors in the water as well as the dinghy but of course our first concern was for the Canso crew' he said.

It was a difficult drop, however, because of the sea conditions and the boat struck the water heavily, breaking its back. Nevertheless it remained afloat and the Canso's navigator, David Waterbury, performed the extraordinary feat of swimming more than 100 yd in the heavy cold seas from the dinghy to the lifeboat, boarding it and paddling it back to his almost exhausted comrades with a single oar. The swim took him twenty minutes, the row back more than an hour.

'We got a great sense of pride and achievement when we saw the aircrew get aboard the boat' David Duthie recalls. 'We also had some Lindholme Gear in the Warwick and whatever we thought of U-boat crews I could not just leave human beings in the water like that so we dropped two sets to them — some were in life rafts, others in life jackets and some seemed to be dead.'

The Liberator remained overhead until RAF and Royal Navy surface craft from Shetland reached the scene. Four of the Canso crew survived but the two who had been badly affected by exposure from the start died. Fifteen of the U-boat crew also survived. The Warwick crew and the Canso survivors later met for what David Duthie remembers was a memorable party. He thinks it says much for the design and construction of the

Lieutenant R. H. Veitch, DFC, SAAF, 260 Squadron Desert Air Force, at a ceremony after the adventures in which his behaviour stood as an inspiration to many other survivors in some other wars.

Airborne Lifeboat that it remained afloat and provided shelter for the flying boat crew in spite of breaking its back in the drop.

On 7 October 1944 a lifeboat-carrying Warwick got into trouble itself in the North Sea. This aircraft had been searching for ten airmen in a dinghy off the Dutch Islands north of Borkum and after finding them and dropping its boat it was attacked by two Messerschmitt 410s. Both enemy aircraft were engaged and one was damaged and driven off. The second EA made nine separate attacks on the Warwick and in spite of violent evasive action its rudder, ailerons, turrets and hydraulics were damaged, the undercarriage dropping down.

The captain ditched downwind into a moderate sea with a six-foot swell and the aircraft broke in two. The crew, two wounded in the gun fight, all got clear. The dinghy did not automatically release and the wireless operator went back in to operate the manual release. One of their own sets of Lindholme Gear was seen floating after the aircraft sank and pulled aboard the dinghy. Their 'Q' type dinghy was equipped with sails which were set and they spread the weather apron over themselves. The wounded rear gunner donned a survival suit from the salvaged Lindholme container.

On the following morning they were sighted by another ASR Warwick which dropped a lifeboat. Unfortunately on this drop the parachutes did not self-release but filled with water and held the boat upside down. The survivors tried to cut the parachute cords clear but without success.

About half an hour later another Airborne Lifeboat was dropped, landing only 15 yd downwind of the dinghy. Indeed at one stage it seemed to the survivors that it was going to land on top of them so they smartly sailed their 'Q' dinghy out from under it, went about in yachtsmen's style and sailed back on the opposite tack to board it. They set the rudder and centreboard, started both engines without difficulty, set a course of 255 degrees and put on the protective clothing provided.

At 15:00 hours a Dornier 18 flying boat accompanied by a Me 410 appeared with the apparent intention of 'rescuing' them and taking them prisoner, but these aircraft were chased away by Beaufighters. Towards dusk they stepped the mast and rigged the mainsail. One engine was shut down to conserve fuel. The following morning they set the foresail.

At noon on their third day afloat they were spotted by yet another ASR Warwick which homed in a Navy rescue motor launch and the crew transferred to it at 14:00 hours 62 miles east of Cromer. They had sailed a total of 152 miles in the right direction, thirty miles in their 'Q' dinghy and 122 in the lifeboat. The crew, who were of course experts in survival and rescue procedures, were highly complimented in the official report which pointed out that those who took the trouble to practise escape drills had a good chance of survival even in the worst conditions.

As the main battlefronts extended to the Middle and Far East and indeed around the world so the air-sea rescue services were extended, many of them joint arrangements with the USAAF and the United States Navy. At one stage in the Mediterranean 323 Wing of Allied Coastal Air Forces could call on Catalinas of the 1st US Rescue Squadron, a lifeboat-carrying Warwick detachment from 293 ASR Squadron based in Italy, Fortresses and Liberators of the US 15th Air Force, RAF High Speed Launches, numerous Royal Navy vessels and some CANTS of the Italian Seaplane Wing.

An important and highly effective ASR organisation was established in Malta at an early stage of the war.

One of the most exciting adventures involving Airborne Lifeboats — really a whole series of them — involved Lieutenant Ray ('Dronkie') Veitch of the South African Air Force who flew Mustangs in No 260 Squadron in the Mediterranean in 1944.

On 2 April he attacked enemy communication lines in Yugoslavia, was hit by flak and baled out over the Gulf of Venice about five miles off the Istria Peninsula. He was able to send a Mayday and a Catalina of No 1 Emergency Rescue Squadron USAAF found him drifting in his dinghy in a minefield. The Catalina, being unable to alight because of the mines, called for help from 293 ASR Squadron, RAF, and one of their Warwicks dropped its lifeboat close to him. Lieutenant Veitch boarded it and steered clear of the minefield in accordance with instructions signalled to him. The Catalina then alighted, took him aboard and returned to base.

Three days later on 5 April Lieutenant Veitch's aircraft was again hit while he was 'train-busting' in Yugoslavia. This time he baled out over the Gulf of Trieste — again into a minefield. He got aboard his 'K' dinghy and an enemy torpedo boat came out from the shore towards him. This vessel was deterred by a Mustang and turned back towards land.

Another Warwick of 293 ASR Squadron dropped him a lifeboat which he boarded. Shore batteries opened fire on him and some enemy naval craft again came out. This time the Warwick's fighter escort opened fire with cannon on the enemy craft and finally a Mosquito sank one of them. The remainder retreated. The Mosquito orbited over Veitch in his lifeboat until nightfall while he started the engines and again steered for the open sea clear of the minefield.

On the following morning a Catalina re-sighted him and gave him a course to steer out of the edge of the minefield. It then alighted in a rough sea and took Veitch aboard.

If this wasn't enough on 30 April Lieutenant Veitch had to bale out yet again south of Lake Marano. The following day an American Fortress dropped him a lifeboat which enabled him to get clear of yet another minefield. On this occasion he was met by an RAF High Speed Launch which took him aboard and towed his lifeboat in. Shortly afterwards Ray Veitch received the immediate award of the Distinguished Flying Cross and resumed operations. He survived the war and died in South Africa in 1979.

Chapter Four
Rescues by flying boats

Although the limitations on flying boats alighting on ocean swells have been referred to, many successful rescues were carried out by the three main types in Allied service — the Sunderland, the Catalina and the gallant little Walrus. Some Catalinas and all the Walruses (as well as their Australian predecessors the Seagull Vs) were amphibious and therefore possessed special qualities for air-sea rescue work.

Curiously, the ability to cope with adverse sea conditions both during alighting and taking off seemed to run in an inverse ratio to the types' size with the Walruses often performing amazing feats in both its elements but the impregnable looking Sunderlands often getting into trouble, partly because of the 'tenderness' of their skins — 3/32 of an inch in some areas — in relation to their all-up weight of about 6,000 lb. In fairness, however, it has to be remembered that most Walrus rescues took place relatively close to shore while Sunderlands were subject to the treacherous effects of long mid-ocean swells often indetectable to their pilots until it was too late.

A wise maritime aviator once pointed out that flying boats were not boats which could fly but aircraft which could alight on and take off from reasonably smooth water — often nowhere near as smooth as the hard surface required by a landplane.

Arguments about the wisdom or otherwise of abandoning flying boat development shortly after World War 2 go on to the present day but one often overlooked factor in their contribution to rescue work was their ability to water taxi for long distances even if damage, overloading or weather conditions prevented them from taking off. Several of the episodes listed below illustrate this special quality and show how good seamanship was as important as good airmanship in such circumstances.

This chapter will be sub-divided into accounts of the life-saving achievements of the three main types in order of size. Because of Australia's part in the evolution of the omnifarious Walrus it is perhaps fitting to begin by relating some episodes from an often forgotten theatre of war, the skies off and over the north-west corner of that continent.

The Walrus's antecedents go back to the early 1920s when a series of little biplane flying boats with 'pusher' engines were designed by R. J. Mitchell (who was of course to achieve immortal fame from a very different looking aeroplane called the Spitfire) for the Supermarine company, at that time owned by Hubert Scott Paine who was as interested in fast boats as he was in aircraft.

The Supermarine Sea Lion, powered by a 450 hp Napier Lion engine, was a Mitchell-refined development of a Supermarine Baby first built in 1918 but not developed. A Sea Lion won the 1922 Schneider Trophy at an astonishing 145 mph. In 1923 the Supermarine company was taken over by Squadron Commander James Bird, a former Royal Naval Air Service officer, and a series of Marks of Seagull were produced on the general lines of the Sea Lion but with landing wheels fitted to make them amphibious. In retrospect they seemed to be the answer to any naval aviator's prayers but these were the days of much confusion resulting from the joint control of the 'Fleet Air Arm of the Royal Air Force' and even after successful fleet trials from the HMS *Eagle* of the day they were rated by the powers-that-were as having 'no potential naval use'.

However, a different view was taken on another side of the world and the Royal Australian Air Force, in full agreement with the Royal Australian Navy, ordered six Seagull Mark IIIs in 1925. A 'mother ship' for them was built, HMAS *Albatross*, a 6,000-

tonner which was the first warship to be built in the Dominion, albeit from parts sent out from Britain.

Both Australian Services were delighted with the little amphibians and put them to extensive use in exercises. In 1929 a broad specification was issued for a replacement and the company, which had by then become Vickers Supermarine, took on the project.

On 21 June 1933 the Type 236 Seagull V first flew from Southampton Water. The last of 790 Type 236s (the nomenclature Seagull V gave way to Walrus first in the Royal Navy and RAF, later in the Australian Services) was still flying on civil charter work in 1966. The Australians bought 24 Seagull Vs and later ordered 37 Walruses. The Fleet Air Arm of the RAF, finally convinced of the type's usefulness after trials aboard HMS *Nelson,* initially ordered twelve Walrus Mark Is then numerous batches of Mark IIs.

The British designation 'Walrus' was announced in August 1935. Although really the same aircraft there were some differences between the 'true' Australian Seagull Vs and the Walruses, the former having Handley Page slots on the upper wings and a different arrangement for the jury struts required to support the wings when folded.

Mark I Walruses were metal-hulled, Mark IIs wooden. They were all powered by various versions of the proven Bristol Pegasus nine-cylinder radial engine; were 38 ft long with a span of 45 ft 10 ins. Their maximum speed was quoted, perhaps rather optimistically, as 135 mph (117 knots). They normally cruised at 90 mph (82 knots). To add to their versatility they could be catapulted from battleships and cruisers and could be rapidly recovered by crane, if necessary when the ship was under way.

The vast majority of British Walruses were operated by the Royal Navy which took control of its own Fleet Air Arm affairs shortly before the outbreak of World War 2 but those allocated specifically to air-sea rescue work became the 'property' of the RAF, a number still being flown by seconded naval crews.

Although there may have been many previous incidents the first records of Australian Seagull Vs and Walruses being used on ASR duties are found in the records of No 6 Communications Unit, RAAF. On 2 May 1943 an aircraft of this unit flew to the Timor Sea to assist the crew of a returning bomber. On 24 May Walrus No *X9520* rescued the crew of a Vultee Vengeance which had crashed at Bynoe Harbour. On 6 July the pilot of a Spitfire was rescued at Peron Island, south-west of Darwin. On 17 September the crew of a Beaufighter which had crashed two miles out at sea at the mouth of the Blyth River on return from an operation were rescued.

On 1 October 1943 an Anson of No 6 CU force-landed on a salt pan on the coast of the Gulf of Carpentaria and sank through soft mud. A Royal Australian Air Force rescue launch from Groote Eylandt attempted to reach the crew but was foiled by breaking seas. A Seagull contacted the aircrew and instructed them how to make their way to a beach. This they did after hacking their way through virgin jungle and the Seagull alighted offshore, bringing them aboard by inflatable dinghy. The seas were still rough and the Seagull's port float was badly damaged during a hazardous but successful take-off.

On 4 December a Beaufighter crashed a mile south of Peron Island. A Walrus (again *X9520)* searched and located wreckage but with no sign of the crew. An empty seat type dinghy was recovered from heavy seas. Two days later another Beaufighter crashed in the same area in similar circumstances. A Walrus of No 6 CU searched and found petrol tanks and a dinghy. An airman was lying up to his neck in water in the dinghy. In spite of rough seas an alighting was made taking advantage of an oil slick from the aircraft wreckage.

The crewman in the dinghy, Leading Aircraftman Henry, had two broken legs and was brought aboard the Walrus with considerable difficulty. During the return journey Flight Sergeant Hunter administered first aid and the casualty was handed over to medical staff at base. Unfortunately he died later that night.

On 23 December a report from Air Operations to No 6 CU said that a Spitfire was lost in the Drysdale area near the border between Western Australia and the Northern Territory. A Dragon aircraft went to the area but the downed Spitfire had been spotted earlier by another search aircraft in a mangrove swamp in St George's Basin. On Christmas Eve the pilot was sighted in a dinghy and was able to signal with a mirror from his jungle survival kit.

It was impossible to drop anything to the pilot because of the tall and dense trees so the search aircraft landed at a nearby Mission Station. A Walrus was then despatched. The Spitfire pilot dared not leave his aircraft wreckage because of the terrain and the presence of crocodiles. The Walrus then alighted on a tidal swamp nearby and picked him up by dinghy. The job was completed just in time because the tide was receding with a range of about 20 ft and the pilot could have been stranded for another twelve hours.

On 14 January 1944 a 'long range' Walrus of No 6 CU flew to Drysdale to attempt the rescue of the crew of a survey DH 84 Dragon on Maret Island in the Indian Ocean. They picked up two of the crew, took off at daybreak and then set down on the leeward side of the island, just clear of coral reefs. Local natives supplied a canoe and after stripping the Dragon of valuable engine parts and instruments and leaving two airmen on guard over the remainder they took off with a total of seven 'souls on board', needing about a mile run before becoming airborne.

No 8 Communications Unit, RAAF, records of Seagull/Walrus rescues run almost concurrently. On 12 July 1943 three survivors from a USAAF B-17 Fortress which had crashed near the Makauna Mission Station were rescued either by a Seagull or a Walrus of No 8 CU. On 17 August 1943 one of No 8 CU's three Walruses made an extensive search for a missing Beaufighter crew of No 30 Squadron, RAAF, near Vivigani Island, without survivors being found.

On 11 September a No 8 CU Walrus set out to search for the crew of another 30 Squadron Beaufighter which had been shot down in New Britain. Although the Beaufighter crew were believed to be afloat in a dinghy the rescue aircraft failed to return and no signals were received.

On 8 July 1945 Walrus *X9515* (Pilot Flying Officer N. W. Agnew) took off from Madang to rescue a pilot named as W. Carter, USAAF, who had baled out of a Lightning in the vicinity of the Karaiari River which was held by the Japanese. The Walrus alighted in the 40-yd wide river and into a five-knot stream amongst logs and floating debris. The Walrus had to stay on the water for about two hours while native scouts they had taken aboard moved through deep grass for some 200 yd to collect the American pilot and bring him to a landing point. The Walrus returned him to base.

The 'Walruses, Walrus or Walri' (according to how pedantic one is about one's grammar) of the RAF Air Sea Rescue Squadrons and occasionally ship-borne ones of the Navy carried out hundreds of successful rescues during the Second World War, displaying not only the aircraft's special qualities but also those of their crews in both airmanship and seamanship. Many of the following incidents were first recounted by Lieutenant-Commander G. W. R. Nicholl, OBE, RN, in his book *The Supermarine Walrus* published by G. T. Foulis in 1966 and regarded as an official record at the Fleet Air Arm Museum. His stories cannot be bettered.

The first of his accounts refers to an episode on 17 November 1942 just after the 'Torch' landings in North Africa. On that day Squadron Leader Patterson and Flying Officer Du Vuyst took off in Hudson No *2500* on an anti-submarine patrol. Fairly early in the evening they sighted a U-boat about forty miles north-west of Algiers. Before they could attack the submarine crash-dived. It later re-surfaced and the Hudson attacked again. This time several of the U-boat's crew were seen to fall overboard. Squadron Leader Patterson started to circle watchfully. A few minutes later another Hudson appeared and made a gun attack on the U-boat. Then yet another Hudson arrived and did the same thing.

The U-boat crew at this stage indicated surrender by waving pieces of white cloth and twelve of her crew were seen in the water. Squadron Leader Patterson was then short of fuel, so returned to base and telephoned the naval authorities. After refuelling he took off again, found 'his' surrendered submarine and started circling it again. He was then joined by a Walrus from the 'Algiers Harbour Patrol' with Sub-Lieutenants Blatchley and Bedford in command. Then a Fleet Air Arm Martlet appeared and gunned the U-boat. It was followed by an Albacore which dropped a torpedo.

Squadron Leader Patterson and his crew watched their 'prize' beginning to sink, but then the Algiers Walrus crew saw a destroyer in the distance and flew over her to signal a direction to steer. Sub-Lieutenant Blatchley, the Walrus pilot, then found that the submarine had sunk with a number of survivors swimming in the water. He alighted into a heavy swell, taxying amongst the survivors and picking up fifteen of them.

Wallowing around in the swell with U-boat survivors crammed into his little hull, hanging on to the wings and sitting on the bows, Sub-Lieutenant Blatchley had only one option open — to sea-taxi towards the destroyer he had earlier located. After five miles of this progress two friendly surface vessels came alongside. The U-boat survivors plus Blatchley and Bedford were transferred and the Walrus was taken in tow on course for Algiers. Sadly, just as they arrived off the port and turned into the narrow swept channel, a heavy wave rolled the Walrus over and she was lost.

On 23 June 1943 No 227 ASR Squadron's detached flight at Martlesham Heath was standing by for the return of the big bombers after a major raid on Germany. Two of the ASR squadron's Spitfires were vectored on two courses and saw an oil patch and a dinghy with nine men in it.

Warrant Officer Greenfield, the pilot of Walrus X9526, heard all about this and was given permission to take off with Warrant Officer Horan (navigator) and Flight Sergeant Leighton (wireless operator). When they reached the area they found that their squadron's Spitfires had already directed an RAF High Speed Launch to the spot.

The survivors from the Fortress, Lieutenants Peele and Barade; Second Lieutenants Williams and Hicks; Top Sergeants Thomson and Osborne, and Sergeants Hatten, Zeigler and Swirz, were all safely landed at Felixstowe by the RAF High Speed Launch. Warrant Officer Greenfield, in response to another ditching report, started a square search in his Walrus but after no sightings landed back at base.

More, however, was to happen that day from the Martlesham Heath rescue base. A further report was received of four Fortresses being shot down and the 227 ASR Squadron

Spitfires were sent off on a search. Walrus X9563, captained by Warrant Officer Ormiston, took off and searched the Kentish Knock lightship area for 45 minutes and after wireless instructions returned to base. At 16:40 hours a report came in that a dinghy had been sighted near the Dutch coast with seven men in it.

Two Walruses were despatched with two Typhoons of 198 Squadron as escort. The Walruses found the dinghy after a short search but the seas had risen and they both had to make heavy alightings. The survivors they found were seven members of the crew of a Halifax. Three of them boarded Walrus X9526 while the others got aboard X9563.

Both the Walruses then had to taxi around looking for some smooth patches to take off from with their heavy loads. Four Spitfires which had relieved the Typhoons as top cover continued to circle overhead. After about half an hour Warrant Officer Greenfield got airborne. Warrant Officer Ormiston, however, with an even bigger load of 'souls on board' was still on the water fifteen miles from the Dutch coast and as the sun set he was attacked by two enemy Fw 190s. The escorting Spitfires engaged the enemy aircraft, however, shooting one down.

After Warrant Officer Greenfield landed back at base the senior pilot of the Detachment, Flight Lieutenant L. J. Brown, took over the Walrus and left for the scene with two Spitfires as escort. The sea was too rough for him to attempt an alighting so he contacted MTB 16 and directed it to the still waterborne Walrus. By this time Warrant Officer Ormiston was having to ask for directions from his own escort because the ten-foot high waves breaking over his windscreen were blinding him. As night fell the MTB took over as escort from the still circling Spitfire.

Early next morning Ormiston's Walrus was out of fuel. The MTB, with some difficulty, got a line across to the aircraft and took both its aircrew and the Halifax survivors aboard. The faithful Walrus X9563 had to be abandoned and the MTB reached Felixstowe at 06:30 hours. However, news reached Flight Lieutenant Brown that X9563 had been seen beaching herself on a shoal. He set out in an RAF High Speed Launch on a salvage attempt and to his delight met up with the destroyer HMS *Mackay* with the Walrus in tow.

Flight Lieutenant Brown first boarded the destroyer and then the Walrus, aboard which he found an officer and two naval ratings valiantly trying to steer her and keep her afloat by bilge-pumping. He re-arranged such matters as the fixing of tow-lines with the benefit of his special knowledge of Walruses' behaviour in rough seas and *X9563* was duly towed into Harwich still upright. In an entirely forgivable piece of exhibitionism Flight Lieutenant Brown then had her engine started and taxied her across the estuary to Felixstowe where she was repaired and went on to serve throughout the rest of World War 2.

Official records say that the story of an ASR Walrus' two nights out in the North Adriatic during the winter of 1943-44 'is of interest to show the durability of these stout rescue aircraft'.

An American Mustang pilot, forced to bale out over the Adriatic, floated down into a minefield. There he sat in his 'K' dinghy awaiting the rescuers for whom he had called before baling out. An air-sea rescue Walrus attached to the Desert Air Force was sent to the rescue. Its crew located the Mustang pilot and succeeded in landing close to him in rough seas. They pulled him aboard but a storm sprang up and they were unable to take off again. The crew kept anxious vigil on the weather, watching out for possible floating mines and keeping an eye on the movements of three torpedo boats, believed to be German, which had appeared on the horizon.

They could not taxi the Walrus to shore in the high waves so they were compelled to ride out the storm until the next morning. Spitfires from the Desert Air Force found them an hour after dawn and directed a nearby destroyer to the spot. The occupants were taken off and the storm-battered aircraft was left to ride the waves until she sank 22 hours later.

On 11 June 1944 Lieutenant Ralston of 369 Squadron, USAAF, had to bale out of his Mustang off Berc sur Mer after attacking flying bomb sites in the Pas de Calais area. Lieutenant A. B. Edgar, RN, attached to No 277 ASR Squadron, was on patrol from Hawkinge in Walrus *HD914* with two RAF Sergeants, both named Smith, as his crew and with an escort of two Spitfires.

They found Lieutenant Ralston's dinghy near the French coast and being blown towards it by a stiff onshore wind which was building up white horses. German anti-aircraft and shore battery guns were firing into the area and alighting was difficult into a rough sea sprinkled with the bursts of exploding shells.

Lieutenant Edgar made a fast approach, got alongside the dinghy and the Sergeants Smith hauled the badly wounded Mustang pilot aboard via the rear hatch. After six attempts at take-off Edgar decided his best course would be to taxy home roughly on the line previously taken by the Dover-Calais ferries.

The Spitfires continued to circle and about three hours after alighting the Walrus was met by an RAF High Speed Launch. A sick berth attendant from the launch managed to climb aboard the Walrus via the wings and struts and gave first aid to the badly injured American pilot. The RAF launch then took the Walrus in tow but on entry to Dover harbour its crew re-started the faithful and salt-encrusted Pegasus, cast off the tow line and taxied up the slipway under Dover Castle in a thoroughly justifiable triumphant gesture.

One of the most spectacular rescues by a Walrus in the Far East occurred in July 1944 when Lieutenant J. Carter, USAAF, had to bale out of his Lightning due to a fuel stoppage near Wewak in New Guinea. His flight commander was just ahead and knew of his problem and he landed in heavy scrub, laying out his parachute as a marker. The area was still in Japanese hands but on the afternoon of the following day two Mitchells located him and a Catalina dropped him blankets and food. The following morning another drop was made.

The only pick-up point appeared to be the Kariwari River, half a mile across swamp land from Lieutenant Carter's position. Flying Officer N. Agnew took off from the theatre Rescue Centre in a Walrus and made a preliminary reconnaissance. He dropped a message to Carter saying he would be back the next day and that a rescue party would try to reach him from the river.

The next morning Flying Officer Agnew took off from an advanced airstrip near the coast with two native boys aboard armed with machetes. He was escorted by two Beaufighters and a Catalina. He made a successful landing on the river, the boys paddled ashore in the aircraft's 'M' type dinghy and reached the survivor a few hours later. The next evening Lieutenant Carter was back at the Madang base.

Perhaps the most dramatic of all the Walrus rescues in the distant theatres of war and one described in detail by Lieutenant Commander Nicholl occurred early in the war when the 7,500-ton Blue Funnel liner SS *Eumaeus* commanded by Captain J. E. Watson was engaged by the Italian submarine *Commandante Cappelini* off Freetown, West Africa, in January 1941. The ship was on her way to the Far East with a draft of about 200 naval officers and ratings aboard plus one RAF Sergeant.

After a ferocious gun duel in which both ships were badly damaged and many casualties incurred the *Eumaeus* was finally sunk by a torpedo from the submarine. A high proportion of her ship's company and passengers were able to board lifeboats or cling to flotsam.

They were located by a number of Walrus aircraft from HMAS *Albatross* then lying at mooring in Freetown Harbour, the first on the scene piloted by Lieutenant V. B. G. Cheesman, Royal Marines. His crew were Petty Officer Knowles as observer and Leading Telegraphist Dale as his telegraphist air gunner (TAG). They saw that the men in the water, some in overloaded lifeboats, others clinging to rafts and wreckage and many wounded, were in desperate straits and first dropped their inflatable dinghy to a group who seemed to be in the greatest need.

They then spotted two lifeboats about two miles away from the main body, one empty the other with only two men aboard who could not row it on their own. Lieutenant Cheesman alighted with difficulty along the line of a heavy swell. He had assessed that he might be able to tow at least one of the precious lifeboats back to the main body. The two men then swam across to the Walrus, not

quite appreciating his intentions. One swam back to a boat but was unable to board it. Lieutenant Cheesman abandoned his plan to tow the boat and taxied back towards the main body, picking up two more survivors on the way.

In the main body the position was critical. The temperature was soaring, there were only two lifeboats, both badly holed and almost awash. In trying to taxy close to one of them the swell swept Lieutenant Cheesman's Walrus down on it, damaging the port float and lower wingtip so that any hope of take-off had to be abandoned.

Another Walrus appeared overhead and Petty Officer Knowles signalled it by Aldis lamp asking for a course to steer back to the abandoned and empty lifeboats. On approaching one of them Lieutenant Cheesman, by then the strongest swimmer of the five aboard, swam across himself with a tow line. Slowly they taxied back to the main body again where survivors boarded the lifeboat and manned the oars to cruise around picking up more of their comrades. Other Walruses appeared overhead and dropped supplies and eventually Petty Officer Knowles, who had for some time perched himself on the Walrus' upper centre section as a lookout, saw smoke on the horizon. Aldis lamp signals were exchanged and two trawlers *Bengali* and *Spaniard* were soon among the survivors picking them up.

Lieutenant Cheesman and Telegraphist Dale stayed aboard the Walrus for a long and uncomfortable tow back to port with constant pumping needed. The last three survivors — the RAF Sergeant and two naval ratings who had drifted away from the main body clinging to a mast — were picked up by a destroyer the next morning.

Once again a fully justified demonstration of the Walrus's ruggedness and the reliability of the Pegasus engine took place. Lieutenant Cheesman and Telegraphist Dale managed to start the salt-encrusted engine by hand after entering Freetown harbour and taxied across to *Albatross* to be hoisted inboard with water streaming out of the aircraft's sprung plates. Out of more than 300 aboard SS *Eumaeus only 23 had been lost.*

*   *   *

The Catalina, PBY or Canso, according to whether it was in British, American or Canadian ownership, was another omnifarious aeroplane, coming in both 'straight flying boat' or amphibious configurations and flown by most of the Allied air forces and navies throughout World War 2. It was a 'general reconnaissance' aircraft with a crew of eight or nine, was powered by two Pratt & Whitney Twin Wasps and was 65 ft long with a 104 ft wingspan. More than 600 were built for the RAF alone and formed the equipment of 23 of its squadrons both in Coastal and overseas Commands. Its strength and healthy power to weight ratio enabled the type to be used in many successful air-sea rescues throughout the world and the following incidents perhaps demonstrate its versatility.

On 20 April 1942 Squadron Leader R. Y. 'George' Powell of 202 Squadron was returning to his Gibraltar base after escorting a naval force in the Mediterranean when his wireless operator picked up a message saying that a Hudson crew had ditched ten miles east of Mellila, a Spanish enclave in Morocco. George Powell was about 100 miles north of the position given and immediately turned back on a reciprocal bearing. In the Mellila area they saw a group of fishing boats approaching port and circled low over them looking for any signs of yellow Mae West life jackets on their decks. (George Powell, now living in Warminster, says that if there had been he would have alighted and taken the wearers off at gunpoint if necessary, even though they were well inside Spanish territorial waters.)

Seeing no signs they returned to the given ditching position and spotted an occupied dinghy on the first run of their search pattern. They alighted and as they were taking the Hudson crew aboard another Catalina which had been sent out 'officially' to effect the rescue appeared overhead. 'We gave them a two-finger salute and took off', George Powell recalls.

On 18 May 1942 a message was received at

An RAF Catalina smoke-bombing during training.

Gibraltar that a Catalina had been shot down by Vichy French fighters off Algiers. Both pilots had been incapacitated but the rest of the crew were unhurt and the boat was flyable. George Powell and his crew set off with the intention of putting a spare pilot aboard and bringing the aircraft back. As they approached the Algiers area they received a return-to-base signal and reluctantly turned for home. On the way out, however, they had seen a destroyer moving at speed on course for Gibraltar and when they caught up with it again they engaged Aldis lamp signals which went:

'Have you the Catalina crew?' Answer 'Yes'.

'How is Bradley?' (Flight Lieutenant Jim Bradley was the downed Catalina's Canadian captain.) 'When do you get to Gib?' Answer: 'Dusk. Can you take stretcher case and orderly?.'

George Powell's answer to the last signal just said: 'Landing'.

He first made a wide circle to jettison his depth charges and by the time he alighted the destroyer, HMS *Ithuriel*, already had a ship's boat in the water with Flight Lieutenant Bradley and a sick berth attendant on board. He had a cannon shell in his abdomen and needed urgent surgical treatment. The boat's crew told George Powell that the second pilot, Stan Sismey (a noted Australian cricketer) had eleven bullet wounds but that they could look after him in the ship's sick bay.

After take off Gibraltar was contacted by wireless with a request for immediate hospital facilities and George Powell wound up his Catalina to her maximum 190 mph, alighted inside the harbour and taxied to a mooring at high speed. An ambulance was waiting and before George had time to leave the flight deck his friend was on his way to hospital. Three days later he was allowed to visit him and Jim Bradley produced a matchbox containing a half-inch piece of shrapnel which had arrived with a clink in his bed equipment, thereby making a second operation unnecessary. He made a full recovery and returned to Canada with a Distinguished Flying Cross.

On 11 June 1943 a B-17 Fortress of 206 Squadron RAF captained by its CO, Wing Commander R. B. Thomson, DSO, sighted

RAF Catalina amphibians on the ground *(RAF)*.

U-boat *417* on the surface north-west of the Faroes. The U-boat was first seen from 1,500 ft seven miles ahead. Its captain, Kapitän W. Schreiner, had apparently seen the approaching aircraft because he began evasive manoeuvres. He then apparently decided to stay on the surface and fight off the Fortress with his guns.

Wing Commander Thomson attacked from 50 ft. Kapitän Schreiner opened fire at 600 yd range and his guns hit Fortress 'R' several times before it straddled the U-boat with five depth charges. Half a minute later the U-boat sank stern first and the Fortress crew saw about thirty seamen in the water shaking fists at them.

During the duel three of the Fortress's engines were put out of action and Wing Commander Thomson was forced to ditch almost immediately. He and his crew of seven escaped and boarded their dinghy but packs containing rations and distress signals were swept away along with the dinghy oars. The Fortress's wireless operator had, however, managed to get an SOS signal off and fairly shortly afterwards a Norwegian-crewed Sunderland arrived overhead and attempted to alight.

An RAF Catalina at Singapore in World War 2. The 'boat handlers' in the foreground were locally recruited *(RAF)*.

An official report says that the sea state was very high and that the Sunderland captain decided prudence was the better part of valour so overshot after making several attempts and sustaining damage. It came to light quite recently as the result of a letter to *Air Mail* (the journal of the Royal Air Forces Association) that the Sunderland captain was Conrad Skjoldhammer, now living in Slependen, Norway.

He recalled in his letter that after having been sent to the area and conducting a square search he and his crew saw men in a dinghy, dropped supplies and then attempted an alighting. His description of what happened illustrates dramatically the problems facing flying boat pilots in such conditions.

'I got the crew into ditching positions and we started to let down. The wind was coming at 90 degrees across tall waves making the sea very rough. Just before we touched down I saw a huge wave coming towards us, high above the windscreen.

'I banged the throttles open and the stick back but the wave hit us with a hell of a bang. The radios fell out of the racks and the whole aircraft shuddered. We were hanging on the props at 58 knots. Somehow we kept flying but we had now lost our long range radio contact and our ASV (Air-to-Surface Vessel) radar had gone.

'We had circled the dinghy for a few hours when a United States PBY 5 (Catalina) from Iceland came to relieve us. The captain told me he was going to try to land. I advised against it but he would not listen even when I told him the sea was much rougher than it looked.

'I followed him down on his approach. He got the aircraft down but a wingtip was caught by the sea and that was that.

'The crew managed to get into a dinghy so now I had two to look after instead of one. We stayed over the dinghies for several hours and were finally relieved by a Hudson from Iceland.

'The crew of the B-17 were later picked up by another Catalina but the crew of the United States PBY were, as far as I know, never found'.

Kaptein Skjoldhammer's account can now be supplemented by others of the same incident.

An official report reads that only one member of the PBY 5 (a United States Navy aircraft) which 'went in' survived the crash and the subsequent exposure and that he was rescued by yet another US PBY six days afterwards.

News of the Fortress crew's ditching reached the Coastal Command base at Sullom Voe in Shetland. After a long stand-by on the third day after the ditching they heard that another Fortress had located the survivors and dropped supplies. This Fortress was able to stay overhead and home in other rescuers.

At Sullom Voe another Catalina (FP 102) of 190 Squadron was prepared for a special task, being lightened by the removal of guns, bombs and depth charges and with its fuel restricted to sufficient for a 750-mile round trip plus a possible alighting and take-off.

A volunteer crew of five was called for (instead of the normal nine) and they consisted of 'time expired men' who had finished a tour of duty at remote Sullom Voe and were awaiting transport to take them on leave. This was agreed upon in order not to interfere with the current pressing anti-submarine operations. The captain was Squadron Leader Holmes, DFC, the second pilot Pilot Officer White, the navigator Flight Lieutenant Harris, the wireless operator Flight Sergeant Button, DFM, and the flight engineer Sergeant Bill Warner.

They took off and found the Fortress survivors in the dinghy fairly quickly with the help of the second B-17 which was still circling the scene. Squadron Leader Holmes and Pilot Officer White achieved a classic 'stalled on' alighting at about 60 knots across a long south-westerly swell. They then carried out a difficult crab-wise taxy to the dinghy. They took the eight survivors aboard (they had been in an open dinghy in hostile northern waters for four days) and after jettisoning some more fuel Squadron Leader Holmes found a flat patch in the swell and took off at about 50 knots airspeed.

Bill Warner, now living in Tonbridge, Kent, remembers it all very well. 'The Catalina was an excellent flying boat for taking off from and landing on rough water' he told me recently. In very rough water the procedure was to make a "stall landing". The pilot held off just above the water and pulled the nose up, at the same time closing the

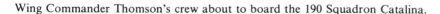

Wing Commander Thomson's crew about to board the 190 Squadron Catalina.

throttles and the aircraft literally dropped in tail first with hardly any forward speed.

'In this incident we landed up-wind of the dinghy, stopped the engines and let the wind blow us back. However, we drifted past it and had to start up one engine and taxy up again as though we were picking up a buoy.' (Bill Warner's personal account tends to make it all sound very easy which it obviously was not! The operation was rated in official circles as a superb example of good and courageous combined airmanship and seamanship.)

In Australia Catalinas were frequently used on air-sea rescue operations along with Seagulls and Walruses in the 'forgotten war' against Japanese off the northern and North West Territories. Some incidents, can be regarded as typical.

Not all were successful. The 'A' crew of 40 Squadron, RAAF, were shot down in a Catalina captained by Flight Lieutenant C. Williams on 15 October over Macassar in the South Celebes. Twenty-four hours later the Japanese propaganda radio announcer 'Tokyo Rose' declared that the crew had received an honourable death, having been beheaded.

On 23 October a 42 Squadron Catalina was hit by anti-aircraft fire while mine-dropping in the Macassar area. The crew, captained by Pilot Officer C. D. Hull, were rescued by another Catalina skippered by Flight Lieutenant Ortlett the following day.

Royal Air Force Catalinas were also often active on rescue missions in the Far East. In early 1945 the SS *Sutlej* was sunk by a submarine, probably Japanese but possibly German at that state of the war, off the Maldive Islands in the Indian Ocean. Eighteen eventual survivors spent seven weeks aboard two life rafts before rescue. In desperate conditions they were found on the 48th day by the crew of Catalina 'T' 'Tommy' *(W8406)* of 205 Squadron RAF, then based in Ceylon.

The then Pilot Officer Stanley Shackleton, now living in Chadderton near Manchester, remembers the occasion well. He recalls that 'T Tommy' was one of the oldest Catalinas in service, carrying an ancient radar set which did not work very well. However, during their search they found the survivors and dropped smoke floats, a set of Lindholme Gear and

Sergeant Bill Warner.

some Thornaby Bags. They could not alight because of the ocean swell conditions but they were able to home in a sloop which completed the rescue.

One of *Sutlej's* engineer officers, Arthur Bennett from Liverpool, recorded in a later newspaper interview that on their 48th day afloat an aircraft circled overhead. His account said: 'At first we thought it was an enemy plane but later we saw the old red-white-and-blue roundels of the RAF.

'He circled around and the crew waved. He came very low dropping stores which we could not make. Soon his fellow planes came and stayed with us about three hours.'

On the 49th day Mr Bennett recalled: 'Our old friend was back there in the clouds. We gave him a flare and over he came and was with us all day dropping stores which I swam for — very foolishly with sharks around.

'Then a sight I shall never forget — a man o'war steaming full speed for us.'

It is perhaps out of survivors' accounts such as this that one can appreciate the real value of an air-sea rescue service anywhere in the world, at any time, in war or peace.

*   *   *

The 'immortal Sunderland' was originally produced as a military development of the Short 'C' Class Empire flying boats designed for Imperial Airways in the 1930s. A total of 749 were built, the basic type remaining in RAF front-line operational service for seventeen years — something of a record until the Shackleton took to the air in the 1950s and stayed in it until the 1980s, of which more later!

Although many of these magnificent aircraft got into trouble and a number were lost in rescue operations, their contribution to the saving and preservation of life during World War 2 and afterwards was enormous. Not only did they carry out many direct rescues involving 'alighting' but even more often they were instrumental in the salvation of torpedoed ships' crews and passengers in the cruel Atlantic War and elsewhere around the globe, by their very presence overhead. References to their part in what can be construed as a life-saving operation — the Berlin Airlift — will be found in a later chapter.

In any comparison with flying boat performances on to, and off, rough seas it should always be remembered that the Sunderland pilots usually attempted their

Survivors from a torpedoed ship in their lifeboat after an 'incident' in the Pacific War. This picture was taken by the crew of a Catalina which found the lifeboat and later arranged the completion of the rescue *(Stanley Shackleton)*.

Stanley Shackleton and crew with their faithful Catalina 'T for Tommy' *(Stanley Shackleton)*.

rescues in the most inhospitable waters — in mid-Atlantic with the huge swells running whereas a lot of the successful Walrus and Catalina rescues were achieved in rather more benign conditions. All things are relative!

A high proportion of the Sunderland rescue incidents described below will refer to those carried out by No 10 Squadron Royal Australian Air Force. There are two main reasons for this. The first is that 'No 10 RAAF' was a remarkable unit. Most of its members arrived in Britain in 1939 to take delivery of, and receive instruction on, the Sunderlands which the Australian government had bought. Having done most of that, the war broke out and they stayed for the duration, supported by many reinforcements from their homeland. They operated for most of the time from Mount Batten, Plymouth, and they made for themselves a well-deserved reputation for skill, gallantry and general *bonhomie*. The citizens of Plymouth will never forget them.

Another reason for a preponderance of Sunderland rescue stories from 10 Squadron, RAAF, is that their records were so well kept, and presented in a book entitled *Maritime is*

Number Ten written and published by Flight Lieutenant Kevin Baff, to whom this author is deeply indebted.

Leaving aside 'No 10' for a moment, however, the first recorded rescue by Sunderlands, indeed probably the first air-sea rescue of the Second World War, took place only a fortnight after the outbreak of official hostilities, when the tramp steamer *Kensington Court* was torpedoed 100 miles south-west of Fastnet.

Two Sunderlands, one from 204 Squadron, the other from 228, already on patrol over the Atlantic, picked up distress signals. The first *PB73* reached the ship ten minutes before it sank. Alighting on a rough sea it took aboard twenty of the 34 survivors from an overcrowded lifeboat. Shortly afterwards the second Sunderland rescued the remainder and both aircraft flew back to base, the entire crew of the *Kensington Court* being back on British shore within an hour of their ship sinking.

In the early years of the war Sunderlands performed enormous rescue feats during the evacuations of Norway, Greece and Crete. During the Crete evacuation in 1941 a Sunderland was reputed to have carried 87 passengers on one flight.

The Sunderlands operated during World War 2 moved up from the Mark I to the Mark V. The fundamental statistics for a Mark V were: length 85 ft 4 in; span 112 ft 9½ in; loaded weight 60,000 lb; maximum speed 213 mph; and power plant four Pratt & Whitney Twin Wasps. Earlier Marks which really bore the brunt of operations were powered by the faithful Bristol Pegasus engines of various ratings.

After several early losses an official Air Ministry Order said that alighting Sunderlands on ocean swells during rescue attempts was 'not encouraged'. It was easy for pilots to underestimate the height of ocean swells, the Directive added, and they would often bounce the flying boat into the air and stall it. The wingtip floats of flying boats were also identified as weak spots. Nevertheless many Sunderland captains, with their crews' agreement, went on attempting such alightings with varied success, rather than leave fellow human beings to die in the sea below them.

On 21 June 1940 Sunderland *N9049* 'B' of 10 Squadron, RAAF, captained by Flight Lieutenant Hugh Birch with Flying Officer John Costello as second pilot, was covering the Dunkirk evacuation. The crew spotted a lifeboat with eight men on board and diverted a British destroyer to it by Aldis lamp signal.

On 23 June 1940 *P9600* 'L' of No 10, captained by Flight Lieutenant Bruce Courtney with Flying Officer Geoff Hayvatt as second pilot, sighted twenty men in a lifeboat. Under Flight Lieutenant Courtney's direction they were rescued by SS *Cap Cantin*.

On 25 June 1940 *P9600*, this time captained by Squadron Leader Charles Pearce with Flight Lieutenant Owen Dibbs as second pilot, investigated an oil patch strewn with wreckage and found two lifeboats in the middle of it. They directed SS *Ainsbury* to the scene and later located three more lifeboats. On 28 July 1940 Sunderland *P9601* 'F' of 10 Squadron, captained by Flight Lieutenant Hugh Birch with Flying Officer 'Attie' Wearne as second pilot, found four lifeboats from the torpedoed *Auckland Star* which had been sunk by the 'ace' Otto Kretschmer in *U-99* eighty miles from Valencia in the Irish Republic. Flight Lieutenant Birch alighted, found that no one in the boats was injured and saw a trawler approaching, so he took off again and returned to base. The occupants of two of the boats transferred to the trawler, the other two reached a British Port unaided.

Flight Lieutenant Birch commented that he felt that in reasonable sea conditions and with proper precautions it was possible for Sunderlands to bring aid to survivors of torpedoed ships in circumstances where assistance from surface vessels might be too slow.

On 25 September 1940 Squadron Leader Bill Garing was flying *N9050* 'D' on convoy escort duty with Flying Officer Geoff Hayvatt as second pilot and they found a lifeboat from the 1,000-ton liner *City of Benares* in mid-Atlantic. The boat was under sail and in the bows the Sunderland crew saw, somewhat to their astonishment, a young boy in full Scout uniform semaphoring in a most efficient manner 'C of B'.

This ship, sailing to the United States with evacuee children and their escorts, had been torpedoed eight days earlier by *U-48*

(Kapitänleutnant Bleichrodt). It transpired that originally 26 people had been aboard the lifeboat including the ship's First Officer (Mr Cooper), six children and their escort (Miss Cornish) and eighteen Lascar seamen. Later they had picked up another six children, two escorts, one adult passenger, a seaman gunner, a steward, a naval signalman and another group of Lascars making 46 in all.

They had linked up at one stage with a lifeboat from another torpedoed ship, the SS *Marina*, but had parted company. They had been trying to sail east, using a tarpaulin to protect the children, and were short of water and food when sighted by Bill Garing and his crew. Bill made three attempts to alight but there was too much swell. He dropped supplies wrapped in Mae West life jackets and returned to the convoy he had been shadowing. He closed up with another Sunderland and between them they guided a destroyer to the lifeboat. The survivors were later landed at Greenock.

At 'first twilight' on 17 October 1940 Flight Lieutenant Ivan Podger flying *P9600* 'E' of 10 Squadron was about thirty miles from a convoy he was escorting off the north-west coast of Scotland when his crew spotted a faint light. They found a lifeboat with 21 men aboard who were survivors from the 5,800-ton SS *Stangrant* which had been straggled from the convoy and been sunk.

Flight Lieutenant Podger made a low pass and discovered that the sea was not as calm as it had looked from a higher altitude. Nevertheless he alighted into a lumpy swell and got alongside the boat. Transferring the survivors via the bow turret was difficult even though they struck their mast. The boat was occasionally running under the Sunderland's bows as both rose and fell in the swell.

Several of the survivors were suffering from exposure and needed hospital treatment urgently. After half an hour of cautious taxying while looking for a flat patch he achieved take-off in a confused swell with breaking waves. He landed the survivors at Oban where they provided information about the probable position of another lifeboat with sixteen on board. They were found and rescued by naval surface vessels.

Understandably, 10 Squadron crews were sometimes in trouble themselves. In June

1941 three Short 'G' Class flying boats owned by Imperial Airways were sent to Mount Batten to be prepared for special long range sorties to the Middle East carrying VIPs. No 10 Squadron RAAF took over their maintenance and provided crew reinforcements.

On 19 June the former 'Golden Fleece', civil registration *G-AFCJ,*, and re-numbered *X8274*, left for Gibraltar with fourteen on board including Squadron Leader Long, RAF, Flight Lieutenant Bowes, RAF, Pilot Officer Jim Barry, Corporal Len Corcoran and Leading Aircraftman Roy Crago, RAAF, Sergeant Hall and LAC Anderson, RAF, with a Brigadier Taverner and two Free French government officials.

Len Corcoran, who was acting as air gunner, related afterwards that at 23:30 hours the starboard outer engine failed while they were over the Bay of Biscay and course was set for Lisbon. They prepared for a crash alighting and the starboard inner then began overheating. They hit the sea hard and Flight Lieutenant Bowes and Pilot Officer Barry were killed instantly. Squadron Leader Long and Len Corcoran were thrown clear and found a dinghy. Although Len Corcoran's shoulder had been broken he got aboard and pulled in Squadron Leader Long, Brigadier Taverner, Sergeant Hill and LAC Anderson. They called out to the others all night but there was no response.

Once they were attacked by a shark which they hit on the nose with distress signal cartridges. Enemy aircraft were sighted on the second day and there was a rain squall on the third night which enable them to collect drinking water in their life jackets. On the fourth day a Heinkel 115 seaplane flew over at 300 ft and was joined by three others. The first then alighted and took them on board.

Len Corcoran — who was promoted to Warrant Officer during his captivity — made one unsuccessful escape attempt during a sort of grand tour of PoW camps which included Stalag Luft 3, the scene of the Wooden Horse saga. He was liberated from Stalag 357 near Hanover by the Royal Scots in March 1945 and was 10 Squadron's only prisoner-of-war.

On 7 July 1941 a Hudson of 206 Squadron, RAF Coastal Command, lost both engines on fire during a 'Crossover' anti-submarine patrol in the Bay of Biscay. Its captain, Pilot Officer Terry Kennan, achieved a dead stick ditching with tail well down — no mean feat in a heavy aircraft with no power at all. Although the aircraft sank in sixty seconds he and his crew, Flight Sergeants Livingstone and Rowley and Sergeant Gibbs got clear and boarded their dinghy. The ditching was made at about six in the morning. They drifted for two days and nights and at noon on the third day they were located by another 206 Squadron Hudson.

Shortly after Sunderland *T9047 (RB-L)* of 10 Squadron, also on a 'Crossover' patrol off north-west Spain with Flight Lieutenant G. R. (Gil) Thurstun as captain, Flight Lieutenant Reg Burrage as pilot and Flying Officer White as second pilot, was diverted to the position and after starting a square search was contacted by the circling Hudson. They dropped smoke floats and studied the sea conditions which seemed reasonable but with an unbroken swell. Flight Lieutenant Thurstun with the full consent of his crew, decided to alight, Mae Wests were donned, depth charges jettisoned and the back end crew mustered on the upper deck.

Reg Burrage later recalled: 'We made our descent towards the dinghy, along the swell and into wind, using two-thirds flap setting. When 30 ft above the water the surface looked quite glassy but the swell was apparent — in fact it looked mountainous.

'This in itself would not necessarily have been a big problem had the swell pattern been regular and the surface ruffled to make it readily visible, but such was not the case.

'We hit the surface fairly hard, the bow turned upwards and we rose about 20 ft in the air. At "Thursty's" request I pushed the throttle levers forward and I thought he intended to remain airborne for a second attempt but he called for throttles back again.

'This time we hit with a jarring impact flat on our belly on top of a mound. This was followed by a few wild bounces and then some wallowing and we were down. Our relief was short-lived!

'The throttles were opened for taxying but there wasn't much response from the port side. I glanced around and noticed something dangling from the port mainplane. It was an oil tank. We then became aware that the entire port outer engine had fallen from the

Sunderland *RB-L (T-9047)* of 10 Squadron, RAAF, after its alighting to rescue the 206 Squadron Hudson crew in July 1941. Note the 'absence' of the port outer engine and the damaged port float, also the dinghies hauled up on to the top of the Sunderland's deck.

mainplane leaving a gaping hole and that the port float was dangling loose. The motors were stopped.'

Some of the crew then adopted the same procedure as that practised back in 1917 by those of the H-12 in the North Sea — they counterbalanced the floatless wing by climbing out on to the opposite one and preventing a disastrous capsize. A wireless report and a pigeon message were despatched, secret documents thrown overboard and three dinghies inflated.

Meanwhile the survivors from the Hudson were trying to reach them, using their boots to supplement their rather ineffective 'glove paddles' without being able to make much progress. One of the Sunderland's eleven-man crew, air-gunner/fitter Corporal Bob Asker, then volunteered to paddle across in one of the flying boat's dinghies to tow the Hudson survivors in. He achieved this difficult task successfully.

The survivors were pulled into the Sunderland's rear hatch — Pilot Officer Kennan had sustained a broken nose in the ditching. A taxying course of 036 degrees True was set, a signal sent to that effect and the four dinghies, two circular, two triangular, put in tow. 'Balancing watches' were arranged so that at least three men were sitting on the starboard wing at any one time to keep the floatless one out of the water.

The second 206 Squadron Hudson which had located Pilot Officer Kennan and his crew continued circling them but had to leave when it reached its fuel exhaustion limit. Reg Burrage recalls they then 'felt somewhat alone'. The weather deteriorated and their good (starboard) float took a pounding with the strut cables being constantly stretched and slackened. The remaining engines tended to overheat and had to be shut down one at a time for cooling-off periods. There was a depressing sight after about an hour — the containers of the smoke floats they had dropped before alighting still floating alongside. The wind had, however, come astern by then so they lowered the flaps to give themselves some 'sail area'.

Some time later the dinghies broke from their tow line. They turned back and recovered a triangular one in which Corporal Asker set off in another paddling expedition

Corporal Bob Asker, RAAF, towing the Hudson survivors in. Note the damaged face of the then Pilot Officer Terry Kennan, the Hudson Captain, in the rearmost dinghy
(Terry Kennan).

this time accompanied by Flying Officer Doug White to tow the others back. This time they lashed the dinghies on to the top of the Sunderland hull rather than risk towing them again.

Two more Hudsons circled them, one dropping a dinghy by parachute which was added to the collection on top of the hull. The weather grew steadily worse but one escorting Hudson remained overhead through the hours of darkness occasionally flashing its navigation lights and finally dropping a parachute flare.

At three in the morning they saw a signal lamp flashing *at horizon level* and eventually the silhouettes of two destroyers were distinguishable. One (HMS *Brocklesby*) drew close and told them by loud hailer that they must come aboard within minutes because she was hunting U-boats. Her captain said he had orders to sink the Sunderland once the rescue was completed.

The destroyer's whaler came alongside while her captain very skilfully manoeuvred the low stern of his ship up to the Sunderland's bows. The flying boat crew and the Hudson survivors grabbed what precious possessions they could (Reg Burrage unscrewed two throttle knobs as souvenirs), left the flight deck lights burning to provide an aiming point for the destroyer's guns and 'abandoned ship', Reg Burrage crushing two fingers in the process between his aircraft's bows and the destroyer's stern.

Brocklesby then stood off at 400 yds and opened fire with multiple pom-poms. These were ineffective but a single round from the four-inch gun set the gallant *RB-L* on fire and she sank. 'A depressing sight', Reg Burrage said. They were all well cared for by *Brocklesby*'s ship's company and stayed aboard her for several hours of U-boat hunting before putting into Plymouth at 11:00 hours.

The remaining members of the Sunderland crew were: Flight Sergeant G. O'Connor (observer), Leading Aircraftmen Jack Drosten (1st fitter), Nicholson (2nd fitter), Donoghue (tail gunner), Arthur Balderstone (armourer), Richard Trenberth (wireless operator/air gunner) and Aircraftman Ted Biggs. All were commended in official reports on the operation, particularly Corporal Bob Asker. (Unlike most operational aircraft in which from 1940 onwards aircrew held the minimum rank of Sergeant, many Sunderland crews, particularly in the Royal Australian Air Force, held the ranks of Corporal and below.)

Terry Kennan survived the war and now lives in Devonshire.

Reg Burrage was soon to be involved in another rescue drama. On 22 October 1941 he and his crew went out to escort a Whitley of 502 Squadron RAF returning from an anti-submarine patrol off north-west Spain on one engine and about to ditch. After square and creeping-line-ahead searches they received a signal from a Hudson which was overhead a dinghy with five survivors in it. They closed up on this and another Hudson and dropped a smoke float near the dinghy. They then received a signal from base: 'Do not land unless conditions permit'.

Reg Burrage's subsequent account of what happened illustrates better than any the problems facing a flying boat pilot in such conditions and how with great skill, they could sometimes be surmounted. He said in an account published in full in *Maritime is Number Ten*: 'I did not find it easy to reach a decision on this matter and there was not a lot

of daylight left. The swell appeared to be fairly moderate by Atlantic standards but most difficult to assess with the wind blowing nearly along it.

'The sea was broken by whitecaps which appeared to be about eight feet from crest to crest. We kept on dropping smoke floats whilst trying to size up the situation.

'We decided to jettison the bombs and depth charges and then give it a go.

'I climbed to 800 ft to release the bombs and depth charges. I made several approaches past the dinghy along the swell, two with flaps down and airscrews in fine pitch but wasn't satisfied with the look of the sea.

'The last smoke float went out the last run but I decided to alight. I could not see the dinghy but approached in the general direction with flaps between two-thirds and fully down.

'I glimpsed the dinghy and realised I had overshot slightly, but kept holding the aircraft off, at about six feet until a "not-so-bad" patch of water came up, and then touched down.

'The initial part of the alighting run from crest to crest wasn't too bad but as she slowed up we were jolted about rather badly. I checked the floats and everything seemed intact so we taxied back about a mile to the dinghy.'

Reg Burrage and his crew found there were six men in a partly waterlogged two-man dinghy and they were unable to manoeuvre it with their paddles. Reg turned into wind, cut his inboard engines and lowered the flaps again, allowing the Sunderland to drift back towards the dinghy. As they drew close he cut the outer engines and ordered the Sunderland's own dinghy to be launched on a tow line with Tom Egerton and Doug White (the latter having had dome dinghy manoeuvring experience in the previous rescue) aboard.

The first tow line was too short so they knotted on an extra length but even so they were short of rope so Reg re-started the outer engines, taxied round to starboard and brought both dinghies alongside each other in a remarkable piece of seamanship/ airmanship. The survivors were pulled in through the Sunderland's aft hatch.

Reg Burrage then decided to attempt a

take-off before the sea-state worsened and the light failed. It was understandably a rough take-off. He remembers he held his wheel hard back, that there were several violent bumps when they hit at least two wave crests and that at last they were airborne. On the way back they sighted an RAF rescue launch bent on the same task. On signalling what they had done they received the reply; 'Blast'.

Flight Lieutenant Burrage's crew on this occasion included Sergeant Bob Smith (observer), Leading Aircraftmen Richard Trenberth (wireless operator), and Russ Mullins, Aircraftmen Ted King (2nd fitter), Harry Rosemond (rigger), Eric Lee (tail gunner) and Jack Spencer (armourer). They later received a signal from the AOC of 19 Group Coastal Command, Air Vice-Marshal G. R. Bennett, saying: 'Well done you have shown great initiative and fine *seamanship*.'

On 12 November 1942 the SS *Buchanan* was sunk by a U-boat in mid-Atlantic 500 miles from land. The first torpedo set her on fire and the second sank her. It took thirteen days for all aboard to be rescued. Sunderlands, Catalinas and Fortresses of Coastal Command flew a total of 55,000 miles on the task.

Much of the air side of the rescue task was carried out by Sunderlands of 220 Squadron, RAF. On 'Day 4' (16 November) a lifeboat with twelve survivors aboard was sighted and its occupants rescued by SS *Lightning*. On 'Day 8' (20 November) another lifeboat commanded by the ship's First Officer was sighted by aircraft which dropped Thornaby Bags.

On 'Day 9' this boat was located again by search aircraft. Two more Thornaby Bags were dropped and a warship was homed in to take the survivors aboard that afternoon. The same day a lifeboat commanded by the ship's Third Officer was sighted by a Sunderland of 220 Squadron. Rations, signal cartridges and charts were dropped by parachute in a bag tied to a Mae West life jacket by the flying boat's navigator, Pilot Officer Robinson.

On 'Day 11' (24 November) the *Buchanan*'s captain's lifeboat was sighted, the occupants holding water cans upside down as a sign of distress. Two Coastal Command Fortresses dropped more Thornaby Bags with tins of water. On 'Day 12' (25 November) HMS

Leamington closed with the *Buchanan*'s captain's boat and took him and another sixteen on board.

The *Buchanan*'s Captain on coming ashore was reported in newspaper articles to have said: 'Thank God for the Navy and the RAF. We stood as one man to cheer those RAF aircraft when they found us.'

In January 1943 Beaufighter *T5112* of 272 Squadron, RAF, ditched 150 miles off Malta. The pilot was Flight Lieutenant Coleman with Sergeant Lynehale as his observer. Both got into their 'K' dinghies and five hours later an RAF Coastal Command Sunderland alighted in a two-foot swell and rescued them both. As the Sunderland was about to take-off the crew saw a Spitfire dive into the sea quite close to them. The Sunderland taxied in search of a parachute in the gathering dusk and they spotted the raised arm of the ditched pilot as he rose on top of a swell. They got him aboard with difficulty. He was lucky to have been spotted because his Mae West was dirty and almost invisible and he had not used either his life jacket whistle nor his fluorescine dye. Nevertheless he was added to that day's Malta Air Sea Rescue list.

On 19 May 1943 Flight Lieutenant Geoff Rossiter of 10 Squadron, RAAF, flying Sunderland *W3984/5,*, closed in on two survivors from a 224 Squadron Liberator which had been shot down six days earlier during an air battle against some Ju 88s in the Bay of Biscay.

Geoff Rossiter first dropped a Thornaby Bag to the survivors and then alighted into a heavy eight-knot swell. His second pilot, Flying Officer Merv Jones, later recorded: 'Down we went and Geoff put down in a beautiful landing. The old swell made the aircraft shudder a lot but we started taxying towards the dinghy which was about a mile off and appearing every now and again on the top of a swell.

'We reached the dinghy and after three attempts I managed to get it alongside the hatch but had to cut all motors to do so. One chap could not help himself at all and had to be carried in and laid on a bunk. He was badly wounded in several places and after six days of absolute exposure without food and practically no water, was just about done.

'The other chap was not wounded but was

very weak and badly burnt. We gave them all the possible medical attention we could, and served hot drinks, then decided to get them home as quickly as possible.

'We knew the take-off would be hard and I don't mind admitting that it had me a bit scared. I started all four motors for Geoff and prepared everything and then we let her go.

'It was rather alarming as we tried to take off along the swell and out of wind, but as she picked up speed she swung into wind, reared up and bounced from the top of one swell to the other at an alarmingly low speed.

'I held my breath for about five to ten minutes and Geoff was working like hell; but after doing this three or four times from one swell to another we managed to get enough speed to climb away.'

The account above again demonstrates in an airman's own words some of the problems facing flying boat crews in alighting and taking-off and may give some food for thought to those who still argue out the landplane versus flying boat theory.

From the middle of World War 2 onwards RAF Coastal Command long range flying boat tasks were supplemented by the work of 'VLR' (Very Long Range) landplanes, many of them Liberators, others variants of the Halifax bomber, together with the Command's Fortresses. As has been indicated, in the air-sea rescue world, it was not only the 'direct' rescues which counted, but the contributions that these aircraft made to the survival of so many torpedoed ships' crews and passengers, especially in the Atlantic but also often much further afield.

The viewpoint of a torpedoed ship's survivor was very well expressed by Captain W. G. Higgs, OBE, Master of the Motor Vessel *Port Victor,* who wrote a letter to the Air Ministry on 20 May 1943. It read:

'Dear Sirs.

'The writer commanded MV *Port Victor* sunk by enemy action 560 nm SW of Cape Clear April 30 1943, survivors from which were sighted by searching Liberator next morning.

'I have already written a letter of gratitude to Flt Lieut J. A. Walker, 86 Squadron, Home Forces and am sorry that I did not preserve a copy to enclose herewith.

'The purpose of the present note is to express our fervent thanks to those at Headquarters who were responsible for the organisation of what I shall always call "The Perfect Rescue".

'Flt Lt Walker's note, scribbled on a page torn from his logbook, hangs framed before me as I write, beneath a picture of my lost ship.

'The sound of his engines was the finest music these ears will ever hear.

'God bless and prosper the RAF.

'Your faithfully

'W. G. Higgs

'(Captain WG Higgs, OBE.)'

A note by the Editor of *Coastal Command Review* read: 'Captain Higgs can rest assured that it is a real, although unfortunately, a rare, pleasure to Coastal Command to have an opportunity of giving direct help of this kind to the merchant seamen of whose gallant devotion to duty we see so much.'

Chapter Five
Into the helicopter rescue age

As World War 2 wore on the demands for rescue services involving aircraft extended from the sea to mountains, deserts and jungles. These demands and the responses to them were to lay the foundations for rescue facilities which were to expand and improve dramatically over more than forty years. Combined with the lessons learned in the wartime air-sea rescue operations they led to the building up of what is unchallengeably the best service of its kind in the world, available to help not only members of the armed forces but (to an even greater extent) civilians in various forms of distress.

During the course of a 'transition period' stretching from the end of hostilities in 1945 into the early 1950s the letters 'ASR' (Air Sea Rescue) were transposed to 'SAR' (Search and Rescue, recognising that aircraft could succour those in distress on the land as well as on the sea.)

Deserts can often be as hostile to downed airmen as seas. In July 1943 a United States Liberator returning from a raid on Sicily lost its bearings over Libya. Ten crew members baled out and descended on to volcanic lava desert about 300 miles south of Benghazi. Their SOS was received and an RAF Wellington plus two USAAF Liberators set out to search, without initial success. Later five survivors were sighted, then a further two, and supplies were dropped. In the meantime a land rescue attempt was organised by a Light Car Patrol of the Sudan Defence Force. The latter was given the position of the survivors but the difficulty of driving vehicles or landing aircraft on the lava was overwhelming. A diary of subsequent events reads:

'13 July: An ASR Wellington dropped further supplies to a group of four survivors. Two Wellingtons and three Liberators searched all day.

'14 July: Two survivors located by a Liberator. Another land patrol requested from Derna.

'15 July: An ASR Wellington took with a composite crew consisting of those who had made earlier sightings. Both parties were relocated about eight miles apart.

'16 July: The land parties struggled on, sometimes having to manhandle large blocks of lava.

'17 July: Land parties reached a rendezvous given them by the Wellington and prepared a landing strip for rescue aircraft.

'18 July: A Wellington and a tiny two-seat Magister trainer managed to land on the strip.

'19 July: The land patrol was guided by the Wellington, first to the two survivors and then to the other four. Two were injured, the others weak but well. They thought the remaining four crew members were somewhere in the "coal" but had no idea of their location. The six survivors were flown to Berka in two Wellingtons and the search resumed, but without success.' The aircraft of what had become the Middle East Rescue Flight flew a total of 120 hours and covered a search area of 15,500 square miles on this operation. The land parties travelled 1,350 miles.

Many aircrews who crashed in the Western and Libyan deserts owed their lives to No 294 Air Sea Rescue Squadron and its predecessor, the Middle East Rescue Flight. A typical incident occurred in May 1944 when a crew of Sergeants crashed into sandhills south-west of Suez while on a cross-country training flight.

On 27 May a Wellington of 294 Squadron located five survivors and circled until relieved by a second aircraft which dropped medical supplies and other comforts. One of the Wellingtons told base that it might be possible to land a light aircraft in the area. The only suitable aircraft available was 294's one and only Walrus which was temporarily

The RAF Sharjah Mountain/Desert Rescue Team on exercise in the Trucial Oman States circa 1970. *(Phil Luff)*.

unserviceable. Ground crews went to work and it was airborne in ninety minutes. It landed a quarter of a mile from the crash scene, thus again demonstrating this aircraft type's remarkable versatility in the rescue role.

Four of the five survivors were seriously injured. A stretcher for one particularly badly injured man was improvised out of a parachute and some engine cowlings from the wreck and all the wounded were put aboard the Walrus which somehow managed to take off with the overload. All but one of the survivors recovered.

Desert rescue techniques were really an adaptation of those used at sea with road or at least 'wheeled' vehicles taking the place of launches. The special skills of the Long Range Desert Group were often utilised to good effect.

One remarkable desert rescue was carried out in 1953 when an RAF Valetta flying from Khartoum to Nairobi had engine failure with seven on board and crash-landed in 'Bad Lands' about 250 miles south of its take-off point. Aircraft from RAF Khartoum found the Valetta and ground parties were organised from relatively nearby villages. The aircrew

and passengers from the Valetta were found, in some *extremis* through shortage of food and water and taken back to Khartoum by camels and donkeys.

Later an RAF ground convoy, supported by the crew of an Anson which managed to land alongside the belly-landed Valetta, set about the task of repairing it and flying it out. Unfortunately records available do not state whether or not they succeeded.

A few years earlier a remarkable *ad hoc* rescue was carried out by some of the remaining RAF elements operating in and around Egypt. In the early summer of 1949 a C-46 passenger aircraft of Mercury Airways got off a Mayday saying there was fire on board, giving a position about 300 miles north of Khartoum. The Egyptian government of the time had no search or rescue facilities but contact was made with an RAF Anson which happened to be in the approximate area.

The Anson pilot (who happened to be the CO of a fighter squadron) managed to fly over the top of the crashed aircraft on his first square search. He landed and found many distressed passengers and the badly burned pilot. He 'lightened' the Anson by taking everything unnecessary out of it, including his co-pilot; distributed what he had got in the way of desert survival equipment and took off with the injured C-46 pilot and as many women and children that he could get aboard an Anson.

On arrival back at Khartoum — then only a staging post — he persuaded the Station Commander to persuade the pilot of a USAF C-47 which happened to be there, to go back to the crash scene. This was duly done and all the remaining survivors were uplifted to safety.

The jungles of the Far East were of course as hostile to airmen and others as the deserts of the Middle East — in many ways more so because of the difficulties of pulling off forced landings and of reaching survivors. Until late 1943 the rescue of aircrew forced to bale out over jungle — virtually the only means of survival — was the responsibility of the Army working in conjunction with the India and South East Asia Air Commands. Much research was carried out by Wingate's Chindits, by Combined Operations staffs and by an Inter-Services Research Bureau, and an RAF Jungle Self-Preservation School was established at Poona where all aircrews were given three weeks' training. Because of the problems of locating survivors under the canopy of 200-ft or more high trees much of the survival training was based on self-help.

Meanwhile back in the United Kingdom the demand for a mountain rescue organisation was growing with a distressing toll of aircraft crashing either on training flights or on becoming lost while returning from bombing missions. This was met in a typically British *ad hoc* manner initially with the formation of a volunteer team at RAF Llandwrog located near to the dangerous terrain of Snowdonia. Formed by the Station Medical Officer, Flight Lieutenant George Graham, in April 1942, it was later expanded into an official organisation under basic principles which hold good to the present day.

In essence the RAF ground Mountain Rescue Teams have always been voluntary organisations with very small permanent cadres of two or three expert officers or NCOs; the bulk of the work being done by ground tradesmen from the Stations at which they are located, who surrender many weekends for arduous training, and who

'drop their spanners' in an emergency to go up into the hills to try to save life. There are still six 'MRTs' in existence. Over the years they have established increasingly close liaison arrangements with the nation's many civilian mountain rescue organisations and naturally they work in harness with RAF and other helicopters.

By the end of 1942 Flight Lieutenant Graham's little team had brought twelve downed aircrew to safety and recovered 35 bodies from eleven crashes in north and mid-Wales. Graham was awarded the MBE in January 1943. By the end of 1944, the first operational year of the 'official' RAF Mountain Rescue Service, 49 aircrew had been rescued out of 226 involved in 54 mountain crashes. Statistically those figures were not all that cheerful and by the sheer nature of things involving the meeting of aeroplanes with mountains, a high proportion of the work of RAF MRTs is necessarily associated with the recovery of bodies. This aspect of the work is, however, always taken very seriously indeed, as is the recovery of evidence from inaccessible places which might provide clues which will prevent the repetition of the accident.

It is necessary now to back-track to the Far East to describe in some detail one of the most important rescues ever carried out by an aircraft. It took place on 23 April 1944 in Burma. Three of General Orde Wingate's Chindits, two wounded, the other ill with malaria, were being flown to a medical evacuation point over Japanese-held territory in an L-1 light aircraft piloted by Sergeant Ernst Hladovkak, USAAF — one of many American airmen acting in support of the British forces in Burma.

Sergeant Hladovkak suffered a failure of his single engine and made a forced landing on a paddy-field in Japanese-held territory. His plight had been noted by another light aircraft, his downing position plotted, and food and water were dropped to the four men over a period of five days and nights. The Sergeant and his passengers had burned the wreckage of their aircraft and taken cover on the side of a ridge.

Among the USAAF units giving air support to Wingate's Chindits was a tiny experimental one consisting of three Sikorsky

M. Paul Cornu with his 1907 helicopter. His basic configuration of a twin, contra-rotating blade design was an advanced one, only perfected many years later and still with some residual perils in spite of its aerodynamic advantages — the former being tragically demonstrated in the Shetlands Chinook disaster of 1986 *(Musee de l'Air)*.

R-4 *helicopters* which had been sent to this theatre of war for battlefield evaluation.

The Sikorsky R-4 was the first practical helicopter to be evolved on the Allied side during World War 2. Those in Burma were designated YR-4Bs — the letter 'Y' meaning that they were still subject to Service Tests, although the USAAF had accepted the type two years earlier.

Lieutenant Carter Harman of 1st Air Commando, USAAF, was acquainted of the plight of his fellow American Sergeant Pilot and the British passengers and he set off from a rear base at Lala Ghat near the Eastern frontier of India on a 600-mile transit flight over mountains rising to 5,000 ft, to the battle zone. At one stage he even tied on an extra fuel tank to the roof of the R-4's cockpit to give himself some extra endurance.

The statistical payload for the Sikorsky R-4 at that time was one passenger. The *winching-*up of survivors by helicopter was something still to come.

Lieutenant Harman flew into Japanese-held territory and lifted out the four survivors of the L-1; two at a time. He and fellow helicopter pilots in 1st Air Commando USAAF then went on to carry out many similar deeds, proving for all time the value of the helicopter as a rescue vehicle.

The invention, or rather the perfection, of the helicopter as a practical flying machine was, of course, to have a fundamental effect on the whole subject of life-saving by aircraft. The helicopter's capability of flying low and slow, and above all of hovering in a stationary position, pointed to it as being the ideal air rescue vehicle. Much more time, thought, and technical development had to transpire, however, before Lieutenant Harman's exploit in Burma was to evolve into the present-day helicopter rescue service in this country and others.

Lieutenant Harman's little Sikorsky R-4 was an example of the first 'working helicopters' to be produced and put into the air outside Nazi Germany. The concept of the helicopter had occupied the minds of aviation pioneers and dreamers from the earliest dreams of flight by man — indeed Leonardo da Vinci drew the design for one in the 15th century. The Wright brothers thought about helicopters, but like many other early aircraft designers became too busy with the fixed-wing flying principle to apply their minds seriously to a much more complicated problem.

Although the first true helicopter, designed and built by M. Paul Cornu of Lisieux, Normandy, flew on 13 November 1907 to an altitude of one foot for twenty seconds, another thirty years had to pass before the concept of an aircraft which could rise and descend vertically and stand still in the air reached the stage of practicality. There were a number of reasons for this. One was that the aviation pioneers of the turn of the 20th century and their military masters during World War 1 regarded *speed* as the main attribute of the aeroplane over any other form of transport. The idea of making aircraft which could fly slowly, let alone stand still in the air and even go backwards and sideways, crossed very few minds as an objective.

The latter was also very difficult to do, and the other delaying factor in the development of the helicopter was the time required to develop lightweight powerplants and lightweight structural materials. Both had to be developed before a form of aeroplane could be built which could 'displace' sufficient air directly beneath it to keep it airborne without moving forward and gaining lift from fixed wing 'aerofoils'.

The design of rotor blades, perhaps better described as 'rotating wings', took time as well, and so did the complicated gearing needed to make them behave in such a way that the aircraft they were supporting could be kept stable. The 'autogyro' emerged first as a practical form of rotating-wing aeroplane. There is still much confusion over the

A Focke-Achgelis Fa 223 'Drache' *(IWM)*.

Igor Sikorsky flying one of his VS 300s on 14 September 1939. The retention of his trilby hat while at the controls was probably a contrived, but convincing, demonstration of the helicopter's potential *(Sikorsky Aircraft)*.

A 'Hoverfly I' (R-4) under trial by the Royal Navy at Gosport *circa* 1945. One is assured that the ratings were only proving the stability of the aircraft, not actually holding it up. The pilot, wearing his uniform cap in the Igor Sikorsky tradition, is Lieutenant Ken Reed, RN, one of the far-sighted advocates for the adoption of the helicopter in the Fleet Air Arm *(Royal Navy).*

differences between an autogyro (only spelled 'Autogiro' when built by Juan De La Cierva or his licencees) and a helicopter. Essentially the former type of rotary wing aircraft depends upon the 'freewheeling' of its blades under the influence of a conventional airscrew or of natural gliding forces, whereas the latter has engine power delivered directly to its rotor blades.

Autogyros can maintain flight at very low speeds without stalling and can land in, and take-off from, very short spaces; but unlike the true helicopter they cannot hover positively, nor move backwards or sideways. They proved to be, and still are, much simpler to build than helicopters so to some extent they 'stole the show' so far as rotary-wing aircraft were concerned in the 1930s.

In the United States in the 1930s, Igor Sikorsky, one-time Russian emigré and designer and builder of very large aeroplanes including the Clipper flying boats for Pan-American, resumed an earlier interest in helicopters — one which he had toyed with and dropped because of more pressing commitments. By 1941 he had a helicopter designated as the VS 300 flying and was able to give convincing demonstrations of its potential with himself at the controls, playing such little tricks as 'spearing' a ring off a pole with a spike attached to the aeroplane's nose. Out of the VS 300 emerged the R-4; the type piloted by Carter Harman in Burma and by many Royal Navy, Royal Air Force and British Army airmen who had an eye to the future in the mid-war years of 1942-plus.

There had of course, been others in the field of helicopter development, notably Breguet in France and Heinrick Focke in Germany. It was the latter who had made the best progress of all. In association with a fellow countryman named Achgelis he produced the Fa-61, a twin rotor helicopter which was flown on fourteen occasions *inside* the Berlin Stadium in February 1938 by Flugkapitän Hanna Reitsch.

The Focke-Achgelis partnership went on to produce twin-rotor Fa 223 'Drache' heavy lift helicopters during World War 2. Apparently only a small number were built, probably because of the necessity for the German aviation industry to concentrate on fighter production. An archive film is held by Westland showing 'Draches' lifting field guns and other heavy equipment in the 1940s and they were undoubtedly the most advanced helicopters in the world at the time. One survived the war and was flown back to Boscombe Down where it crashed during trials.

No records are extant of German helicopters carrying out rescue tasks although William Green in *Warplanes of the Third Reich* records that SS Hauptsturmführer Otto Skorzeny planned to use one for the snatching of Mussolini from the Gran Sasso Massif in 1943. It went unserviceable the night before the coup, however, and he used a STOL Fieseler Storch instead.

Sikorsky R-4s, having proved themselves in various demonstrations circa 1942 to be the only practical helicopters available to the Allies, were ordered in quantity by the British government. A total of 240 (given the British name of 'Hoverflies') were initially ordered for the Fleet Air Arm in the late 1940s although in fact only 45 were delivered before the end of hostilities.

Of the British Services it was the Navy which took the lead in assessing the potential of the helicopter, with the predecessors of the Army Air Corps (the Royal Artillery's Air Observation Post organisation) also taking a great interest, and the RAF only showing mild curiosity in this ugly form of flying machine — with the notable exception of a handful of far-sighted but relatively junior officers.

The Navy not only visualised the helicopter's potential as a fleet spotter which could take off from, and alight on, the decks of quite small warships but as a rescue vehicle for the crews of its fixed-wing aircraft which

The first recorded winching exercise by a helicopter. The pilot of the R-4 is Commander Frank Erickson, United States Coastguard, who had earlier flown the first known life-saving mission by helicopter, taking blood plasma through snowstorms and high seas to the 100 injured in an explosion aboard a US destroyer off the Jersey coast in 1944 *(Sikorsky Aircraft)*.

all too often went over the side of carriers. The prompt rescue of valuable aircrews had been carried out with reasonable efficiency by attendant destroyers or by Walruses and Sea Otters but the helicopter — albeit one with a better payload than the R-4 — obviously offered a better answer to this problem.

The R-4 Hoverflies with a maximum loaded weight of 2,530 lb and a payload of one passenger or crewman were initially used for fairly mundane tasks such as practice torpedo tracking and VIP transport but the Navy gained much experience with them. A winch system was fitted to an R-4 by the United States Coastguard service which just managed to lift a man in a bathing suit.

As expected, improvements on the R-4 soon emerged from the Sikorsky stable and on 29 November 1945 an R-5 made history by winching up two men who had been clinging to a barge breaking up on a reef in Long Island Sound. The R-5 was piloted by Dmitry ('Jimmy') Viner, Sikorsky's chief test pilot at the time, with Captain Jackson Beighle, USAAF, operating the power-driven 'hoist'. It was an historic occasion, the first of many thousands of helicopter rescues by winch gear.

The R-5 and another improvement designated the R-6 were only interim types, however, and it was the emergence of the Sikorsky S-51 ('Dragonfly' in British parlance, especially after being built under licence by Westlands) which was to change the whole concept of rescue by helicopter.

The S-51 was a really practical helicopter, providing enough lift to support a pilot, a crewman, winch gear and perhaps one or two passenger/survivors, dependent on fuel load at crucial times. It was fitted with a winch which could be operated either by a crewman or directly by the pilot via a button on his control column. The S-51 became the first true rescue helicopter and of course performed many other roles besides.

Dragonflies built in Britain by Westland under Sikorsky licence were powered by 550 hp Alvis Leonides engines, had a loaded weight of 5,500 lb, a cruising speed of 85 mph and a maximum speed of 103 mph. Importantly, they could carry a two-man crew plus one passenger or could be flown single-handed by a pilot who could himself

The Sikorsky R-5 winching up one of the men stranded aboard a barge in Long Island Sound on 29 November 1945, the first recorded rescue by helicopter winch or 'hoist' *(Sikorsky Aircraft)*.

operate the winch and lift up to two survivors with it, via a button on his control (cyclic-pitch) column, known as the 'joystick' or just 'the stick' in fixed-wing parlance.

The full value of the S-51 Dragonfly in the rescue role was dramatically proved in 1947 when the aforementioned 'Jimmy' Viner and Jackson Beighle, accompanied by Lieutenant (USN) Joseph Rullo, were demonstrating one to the American Fleet aboard the carrier *Franklin D. Roosevelt* in the Caribbean. As a 'sales demonstration' things could not have gone better.

A total of six aircrewmen were rescued by the Sikorsky team flying S-51 No *NC92807*, including Lieutenant-Commander George R. Stablein whose Helldiver stalled in on a landing approach and who was plucked out by the helicopter crew while about to go down for the third time.

From 1949 onwards the 'Malayan Emergency' became an increasing commitment for the British Army, the RAF and to some extent, the Royal Navy. One of the special aspects of this long drawn-out campaign against Communist influence in the

Far East was the necessity for very small parties of soldiers to penetrate into jungle territory on foot. As ever, resilient British soldiers took to this form of martial art but perhaps their greatest fear was that of being wounded, accidentally injured or taken seriously ill days away from medical aid. Most old soldiers will admit to this being the greatest of the fears, often transcending that of death.

For the troops involved in the Malayan campaign patrols there were no Red Cross-marked ambulances at hand, nor the chain of first aid posts, casualty clearing stations and field hospitals which had existed even in the desert and jungle wars between 1939 and 1945. If they got hurt or were taken ill the only succour could come from their own medical orderlies or 'evacuation' by stretcher on foot at the rate of about half a mile a day at best. This problem, a crucial one so far as morale was concerned, was recognised, and some old Far East hands in high places recalled the work done by the R-4 helicopters in Burma only a few years earlier.

The case for a helicopter casualty evacuation service was put, but by the time it reached Whitehall the RAF had no suitable aircraft of this type available. However, the Navy released three of its first batch of Westland-built Sikorsky S-51 Dragonflies, and a remarkable little organisation styled The Far East Casualty Evacuation Flight was created on 1 May 1950.

In its three years of existence this little Unit extracted 265 wounded or sick soldiers from the Malayan jungle, flying in hazardous conditions which included temperatures of up to 100°F; humidity of up to 100 per cent; high ranges of hills, dense rain forest trees of up to 200 ft in height and frequent tropical thunderstorms.

Although the Dragonflies came out to Malaya with winches fitted it was soon obvious that their use would not be practical in clearings between trees of the height of Nelson's Column so this form of equipment was removed, thereby saving about 100 lb of liftable weight.

The helicopters were almost invariably flown single-handed so that a reasonable payload remained to uplift casualties and a remarkable liaison arrangement was achieved

with the Army pilots of the Austers of No 656 Air Observation Post Squadron — 'old Malayan hands' who had the reputation of knowing every single rain forest tree by sight. The officer and Sergeant pilots of the Austers acted as navigational pathfinders and with their long-range Army 62-Sets frequently provided the necessary radio communications.

In 1953 the unit was expanded to become No 194 Squadron, RAF, and its Dragonflies were supplemented by some Bristol Sycamore helicopters which had a payload of three passengers while being flown by a two-man crew. The helicopter rescue facility in the Malayan campaign was further enhanced in 1952 when No 848 Naval Air Squadron of the Fleet Air Arm arrived with Sikorsky-built S-55s. The S-55, which later took on the immortal name of 'Whirlwind' when built

The Royal Navy's S-51 'Dragonfly' helicopters operated with a two-man crew and normally had a payload for one passenger or survivor. The inventive Lieutenant John Sproule, RN, devised the 'Sproule Net' by which survivors could be scooped out of the water. Several operational rescues were carried out successfully by this means and a version of the device is still carried in some RN rescue helicopters though now normally only used for the recovery of dead bodies or other objects (RN).

A Dragonfly of the Far East Casualty Evacuation Flight descending into a jungle clearing in Malaya. The 'funnel' effect of clearings amongst 100-ft-plus high trees demanded everything that the Dragonflies and later, Sycamores, had got in the way of power
(Wing Commander J. R. Dowling/British Rotorcraft Museum Archives).

under licence by Westland, became the prime all-purpose helicopter for many years.

The main role for 848 Squadron was troop-carrying but the unit also clocked up more than 500 casualty evacuations in Malaya by the end of 1954. When the long drawn-out 'Malayan Emergency' finally closed in 1960 more than 5,000 rescues and casualty evacuations had been carried out by helicopters.

The Malayan Emergency Campaign was, of course, overlapped by the 'big gun war' in Korea and during the latter conflict several hundred soldiers, airmen and sailors were lifted to safety by helicopters, nearly all of them flown and operated by the United States Navy and Air Force. Indeed, the helicopter's potential as a life-saver was brought home to the public at large by a book and a film called *Bridges at Toko-Ri*. In the film Mickey Rooney starred in the real-life role of one Chief Aviation Pilot (non-commissioned) Durne W. Thorin who, among other things,

rescued no fewer than 118 officers and men from a beached frigate in his S-51.

The last recorded operational rescue by a flying boat (actually a Sea Otter, the successor to the Walrus in the Fleet Air Arm) also took place during the Korean War on 19 July 1950. I am indebted for the details to the former Chief Petty Officer Gilbert O'Nion, the navigator of the aircraft.

CPO O'Nion and his pilot, Lieutenant Peter Cane, RN, were briefed on board their ship HMS *Triumph* that a United States Navy Corsair had been shot down by ground fire off the Korean coast and about 120 miles north-north-west of their carrier's position. By the time they took off from *Triumph*'s deck they had learned that the Corsair pilot, Lieutenant Wendell Munce, USN, was in his dinghy with his aircraft sunk and was being circled by two other aircraft from his own unit.

Lieutenant Cane and Mr O'Nion were warned that sea conditions would be rough for alighting, but they nevertheless established RT contact with the circling Corsairs. By the time they found the dinghy visibility was poor, there were white horses on the sea surface, and conditions were well below those recommended for a Sea Otter alighting. Some discussion took place about the advisibility of alighting but they agreed that a man's life was at stake so they tried it.

Gilbert O'Nion recalls: 'We hit the first wave with a hell of a bang and I thought we would dive into the next one, but with consummate skill Lieutenant Cane held the nose up and after about the fourth or fifth wave we settled into a trough.'

They managed to get alongside the Corsair pilot, Mr O'Nion hauling him on board through the aft hatch, then sinking the dinghy with his knife.

The take-off was difficult, of course. Mr O'Nion again recalls: 'I cannot remember how many waves we hit. It felt like being in a roller coaster at a fairground. Seas were breaking over the top mainplane and the engine, which spluttered and caught again. The last wave we hit pushed us staggering into the air.'

An S51 of the United States Navy operational during the Korean War *(Sikorsky Aircraft)*.

During the Malayan campaign a device called 'The Moses Basket' was made locally to carry casualties in helicopters *(J. R. Dowling/BRM)*.

Chief Petty Officer Gilbert O'Nion in the act of 'hooking up' his Sea Otter. This picture illustrates the perilous, not to mention cold, task, which fell to Sea Otter aircrewmen, marginally worse than that of their Walrus predecessors who were at least out of the slipstream with the former 'pusher' arrangement.

CPO O'Nion in 1948.

Finally they had to contend with a difficult landing back on *Triumph*'s deck. The ship had already landed on its Seafires and Fireflies which were all ranged forward so that the crash barrier had to be kept up when the Sea Otter arrived. It never was, of course, funny for the pilot of a Sea Otter or a Walrus for that matter, to land on to a carrier with the crash barrier up since the aircraft design placed the cockpit almost in the nose, thus ensuring that the pilot would probably be decapitated on impact. However, Lieutenant Cane did it neatly. He was awarded the American Distinguished Flying Cross and CPO O'Nion was Mentioned in Despatches.

The public is still reminded of the helicopter's role in casualty evacuation by the opening shots of the apparently immortal 'MASH' television series originally set in a Korean war situation.

The first full helicopter squadron to be established outside the United States was the RN's No 705 Naval Air Squadron, formed in 1947 at Gosport. Five years after its creation it was to demonstrate to the world the value of the helicopter as a *civilian* life-saver.

On the night of 31 January/1 February 1953 extraordinary weather conditions in north-west Europe resulted in devastating floods in Holland and along the east coast of England. The Dutch government appealed to all neighbouring countries for help, particularly in the form of helicopters. The whole of No 705 Naval Air Squadron with its entire operational strength of nine Dragonflies responded.

In two waves the single-engined Dragonflies crossed the North Sea in blizzard conditions and without escort, and went to work lifting people from rooftops, flooded fields, boats and dykes. They were reinforced by some of the relatively new Bristol Sycamores from the Bristol Company's test-and-demonstration fleet, from the Ministry of Supply's Boscombe Down Experimental Establishment and from the Army's Experimental Helicopter Unit.

The first of British European Airways' helicopters — a Dragonfly piloted by the company's future boss, Captain John Cameron, also arrived, plus others from Belgium and from United States' bases in Europe. In fact every helicopter available in Western Europe converged on Holland to try to help.

The fifteen British helicopters lifted more than 800 people to safety, the 705 NAS Dragonflies with a manufacturer's recommended payload of three persons sometimes lifting six at a time. In addition the helicopters ferried doctors, nurses, medical supplies and food out to remote areas. It was sometimes necessary to drop police and army officers first to encourage frightened civilians to entrust themselves to these strange looking flying machines, the like of which few of the distressed Dutch people had ever seen before.

In the year 1953 another momentous step forward was taken with the re-formation of No 275 Squadron, RAF, in the Search and Rescue role. This squadron, part of Fighter Command, was initially based at Linton-on-Ouse and was equipped with a mixture of Sycamore and Navy-borrowed Hiller helicopters, plus an Anson for general purpose work. Two years later No 22 Squadron was re-formed by Coastal Command at Thorney Island in the same role

A Supermarine Sea Otter. Designed as a successor to the Walrus, it actually made its first flight before World War 2 in August 1938 and entered service from 1943 onwards. It was the last biplane in any category to enter service with the RAF. It differed markedly from the Walrus in that its 855 hp Bristol Mercury XXX was a 'tractor' rather than a 'pusher'. It was specifically developed for air-sea rescue work and many operated in this role in the Far East. Production totalled 290 *(RN)*.

A Dragonfly of No 705 Naval Air Squadron during the Dutch floods *(The Times)*.

and equipped with piston-engined Mark 2 Whirlwinds (S-55s).

Number 275 Squadron was later re-numbered 228 and finally 202 and an early deployment put detached Flights of 22 Squadron down the west coasts of Britain, those of 275 and its successors down the east side. Each Flight, usually consisting of two aircraft with enough crews to maintain a 24-

A member of the crew of the North Carr lightship being winched up by a Sycamore from RAF Leuchars in December 1959 *(Daily Mail)*.

hours-per-day, seven-days-per-week standby, was located on, or near to a major flying training base, the prime role being then as it still is, the rescue of *Service* aircrews in trouble.

Three incidents between 1953 and 1955 foreshadowed the role which helicopters of the Armed Forces were to play in the rescue of *civilians,* however.

In May 1953 Mr David Kaye of Newcastle-upon-Tyne fell while climbing rocks on a tide-washed islet in Kynance Cove, Cornwall, and sustained severe head and leg injuries. The senior Coastguard in the area who went to help knew of the presence of helicopters at the nearby Culdrose Royal Naval Air Station and semaphored with his white cap top to shore asking for one to be sent. In about half an hour a Dragonfly arrived with a surgeon officer on board and Mr Kaye was winched up into the aircraft in a stretcher and taken to hospital where he made a full recovery.

In late November 1954 storm to hurricane force winds struck southern Britain and among other things they caused the South Goodwin Lightship to drag her moorings. At dawn on 27 November 1954 the vessel could be seen on her beam ends on the Sands she guarded with no sign of life aboard. Lifeboats and fixed-wing aircraft did their best but most hope for survivors had been given up when an H-19 (USAAF designation for a Whirlwind) from the 66th Air Rescue Squadron at

Flying Officer N. B. Williams who had had to eject from his Hunter off Flamborough Head in July 1956 being helped out of the 275 Squadron Sycamore which picked him up. This was the first recorded rescue of a fast jet pilot in trouble by helicopter. The helicopter pilot was Flight Lieutenant Thompson with Flight Sergeant McGregor as crewman.

Mr David Kaye being winched up to the Culdrose Dragonfly in 1953. The white cap top of the Coastguard used to semaphore for helicopter assistance can be seen at the bottom of the picture — perhaps 'touched-in' a little!
(Daily Mail)

Manston was able to fly as the wind speed dropped from 60 knots to about 35. A man wearing pyjamas was seen clinging to the deck just below the light tower.

The H-19 crew, consisting of Captain Curtis E. Parkins (pilot), Major Paul R. Park (navigator), Captain Willis R. Kusy (winchman) and Airman 1st Class Elmer H. Vollman (winch opeator and medical attendant) lifted the sole survivor to safety. He was Mr Ronald Murton, a Ministry of Agriculture scientific officer who was aboard the vessel to record the movements of bird flocks as part of an investigation into the carrying of foot-and-mouth disease. He was the first British civilian to be winched to safety by a helicopter in extreme weather conditions. He died as a result of illness in 1979.

On 8 August 1955 Mr Robert Read and his ten-year-old son David, holidaying in a caravan at Cuckmere Haven near Beachy Head, Sussex, went out in a small boat and were washed under the cliffs by a rising tide and freshening on-shore wind. Policemen watching from the cliff top knew about the helicopters of 22 Squadron and asked for their help. Flight Lieutenant Keith Paynter

with Aircraftman Williams as his crewman arrived in a Mark 2 Whirlwind. A direct winching operation was impractical but Williams went down on the cable, waded ashore, put the strop over David Read and saw him winched safely up. He then repeated the process for Mr Robert Read and both were deposited on the cliff top alongside a police car.

Those three incidents, the first of thousands, gave the Fleet Air Arm, the Royal Air Force and the USAAF in Britain much favourable publicity at a time when the noisy and costly flying Services were not all that popular in peacetime Britain. They also marked the emergence of a new breed of aircrewmen — the winchmen — who were to earn much well-deserved glory in years to come.

Service chiefs saw no reason to discourage the continuing requests for help made by the Coastguards and police. Even on cost grounds it was effective to regard such operations as excellent training — far better in fact than practising with oil drums and dummies — and the job satisfaction they brought acted as a good morale-builder.

In the mid- and late 1950s publicity tended to be focussed on the RAF Search and Rescue Flights, all eventually equipped with yellow-painted Whirlwinds, but the Navy was playing its part too in the build-up of a comprehensive rescue service covering the

This picture shows an especially tragic incident which occurred in 1958 when Commander Desmond Russell, CO of 803 NAS 'went over the side' from HMS *Victorious* in his Scimitar, during a demonstration. He can be seen in his cockpit and the winchman from the piston-engined rescue Whirlwind is on his way down, but only equipped with an axe to effect the rescue. The aircraft finally sank and the winchman, Leading Seaman Robert Brown, could not reach the pilot in time.
This incident acted as a 'catalyst' to the provision of diving equipment and diver cross-training for Fleet Air Arm rescue aircrewmen and to the provision of barometrically operated ejector seats in FAA aircraft. Later inquiries proved that Commander Russell had been unable to free his leg-restraining straps in time to get clear of his cockpit. The lessons learned from this tragedy led to the saving of many more lives in subsequent years.

whole of the British Isles. The Fleet Air Arm had by then also acquired a substantial fleet of Whirlwinds, some based on carriers as 'ships' guards' with the specific role of picking up the crews of aircraft which might go over the side, others with a specific SAR role based ashore at Royal Naval Air Stations such as Lee-on-Solent, Culdrose and Lossiemouth.

The philosophy on helicopter rescue has always differed slightly in the two Services for good reasons. In the Fleet Air Arm all helicopter crews are fully trained in SAR techniques even though their primary role may be submarine hunting. Some, particularly winchmen who are cross-trained as divers, do tours of duty as SAR specialists either ashore or afloat. In the RAF the 22 and 202 Squadron crews tend to 'stay in the business', some of them for the whole of their careers. (Crews of RAF 'Support' — troop and supply-carrying — helicopters are, however, also capable of carrying out SAR tasks although not all aircraft are fitted with winches.)

By the turn of the 1950s/60s decade records were showing that something like 1,000 civilians a year were being aided by Service helicopters in and around the United Kingdom. The statistics have to be viewed with some caution and none of those concerned make positive claims of 'lives saved' because many of those lifted by helicopter might eventually have been saved, perhaps in less comfort or indeed in considerable distress, by surface craft on the sea or by ground parties in the mountains.

In the 1950s too many of the first peacetime gallantry awards of the era were made to helicopter rescue crews, particularly to winchmen. The first recipient of such an award was a National Service Aircraftman 2nd Class. He was Raymond Martin of 22 Squadron, who was awarded the George Medal after jumping into a Whirlwind at short notice to act as a winchman and going down on the wire to rescue a couple from a yacht in distress off Hayling Island in June 1956.

Although some Sycamores remained in SAR service for several years it was the Mark 2 Whirlwind powered by a single 600 hp Pratt & Whitney R-1340-40 which bore the brunt of the work. It had a loaded weight of 6,800 lb, a range of 360 miles, a cruising speed of 85 mph and a maximum of 110 mph at sea level. It normally flew with a crew of three and had a maximum payload of eight adults according to fuel state. Staunch and reliable though these aircraft were they obviously required support from fixed-wing aircraft in the form of top cover even when operating under their theoretical limit of fifty miles from shore. The part played by fixed-wing aircraft in the whole SAR structure up to the present day is often overlooked.

Towards the end of World War 2 Coastal Command's Sunderland and Catalina fleets were increasingly supplemented by VLR (Very Long Range) landplanes, notably Liberators and Halifaxes. The carrying of airborne lifeboats was extended from the Hudsons, Warwicks and Fortresses to special Marks of Lancaster (ASR 3s) which remained

Aircraftman Raymond Martin, GM, RAF. A well-deserved award since he had little or no knowledge of 'the situation ahead' of him *(Press Association)*.

A piston-engined Mark II Whirlwind demonstrating its rescue potential in August 1955. Unfortunately seconds after this picture was taken the aircraft crashed, happily without loss of life or injury *(PA)*.

in service well into the 1950s as Coastal Command's responsibilities over the Atlantic continued with the formation of NATO and the constant threat from the east. Search and rescue responsibilities of course also remained heavy in the Middle and Far East.

By 1951 the Shackleton had emerged as Coastal Command's key aeroplane and some of the prototypes were fitted with Saunders-Roe Mark 3 Airborne Lifeboats, as were some of the batch bought by the South African government. However, in peacetime conditions the necessity for survivors to move themselves away from enemy coasts and minefields no longer existed and the well-

proven Lindholme Gear was obviously a more economic type of equipment to carry, particularly since it could be loaded into almost any type of medium or large aircraft.

Survivors of almost any disaster at sea supplied with Lindholme Gear should be able to exist in reasonable comfort and safety for hours or even days until surface ships or possibly long-range helicopters reach them, so Air Commodore Waring's improvisation of 1942 has remained one of the greatest life-savers of all.

The main roles for large fixed-wing aircraft in the search and rescue scenario (in the United Kingdom Maritime Reconnaisance Shackletons and later Nimrods) have been and still are:

1. Deep search. Large Maritime Reconnaissance aircraft with the primary role of submarine hunting and killing have the range and equipment to 'search and find' over vast ocean areas. Modern equipment can indeed pinpoint even a single human head. With their large crews, providing a dozen pairs of Eyeballs Human, Mark 1, they are ideally suited to this task.

2. 'On Scene Commander' or 'Scene of Search Commander'. With their wide range of communications equipment and long endurance these aircraft can, and frequently do, sit overhead the scene of a disaster with their captains able to home in surface craft and helicopters, sometimes acting as flying air traffic controllers.

3. Top cover for helicopters. Even modern twin-engined helicopters in the Sea King/S-61 class can get into trouble over the sea and their crews take much comfort from the presence of a Nimrod in the vicinity of their operations.

4. Direct Aid. Long range MR aircraft can

Coastal Command Liberators *(IWM)*.

A Mark III Shackleton of 201 Squadron *(RAF)*.

An 'MS 9' dinghy inflated and with protective cover up. This type of dinghy still forms the 'heart' of the Lindholme Gear *(Bruce Robertson)*.

often provide direct aid by dropping Lindholme Gear or other types of equipment to survivors of disasters outside the range of helicopters. Even within the range of large helicopters this direct aid can often be vital in terms of time, particularly if survivors are in danger of death from cold and exposure.

A recent classic example of this capability followed the downing of the Air India Jumbo well out in the Atlantic when a Kinloss-based Nimrod was overhead bodies and life rafts less than an hour after the airliner had disappeared from radar screens. Had anyone survived the impact and the presumed earlier explosion they would have been able to board Lindholme Gear to await rescue by surface vessels or the helicopters which were able to reach the scene after refuelling on the Irish coast.

An earlier example of the MR aircraft's direct aid capability occurred when the Greek cruise liner *Lakonia* caught fire 500 miles west of Gibraltar in December 1963. A Shackleton of No 224 Squadron based at Gibraltar and piloted by the now Air Commodore David Leppard was able to drop two sets of Lindholme Gear to burned and injured survivors and the crew saw some climb aboard one of them. During an eleven-hour sortie they also carried out the 'Scene of Search Commander' role and the final death toll of 128 out of 1,032 aboard would probably have been much higher but for their efforts.

Other rescue techniques advanced rapidly in the 1950s and 1960s. The rather serious toll of the first generation of RAF fast jet pilots on training exercises was slowed down if not quite halted by two inventions — the Martin-Baker ejection seat and various forms of what is now known as the personal locator beacon.

The first of the latter, known as 'SARA' (Search and Rescue Aid) was really 'begat' by the 'WALTER' device of World War 2 described earlier, but was compact enough for an airman to carry on his person. 'SARA' was followed by 'SARBE' (Search & Rescue Beacon') and later by even more sophisticated devices which among other things operate automatically upon ejection and which are linked to a world-wide satellite communications system.

A properly equipped combat aircrewman, leaving his aeroplane almost anywhere in the world, *should* be found and rescued within a matter of hours.

A legendary, but probably accurate, story is told in RAF circles about an early rescue exercise in the Libyan Desert circa 1961 in

The burnt out Greek liner *Lakonia* photographed by R.D.P. Milwright, the navigator of the Shackleton which dropped Lindholme Gear to survivors.

which 'SARA' beacons were sprinkled around the then RAF base at El Adem. The idea was that the SAR helicopters should find them, plot their positions and bring them back, thereby scoring exercise points.

A passing Bedou spotted one from camel saddle altitude and full of curiosity picked it up and took it into his tent. The next morning, at first light, he was convinced of White Man's Magic when there was an appalling noise outside his tent, a local sandstorm, and a young RAF Sergeant walked in, picked up the curious object and said: 'I'll have that if you don't mind. I think it belongs to us.'

Much more recently a Sea King responding to a rescue beacon signal which had been received via satellite at the International Co-ordination Centre in southern France found itself hovering over a Glasgow housing estate with a very precise position signal being emitted from one particular dwelling. A little later the embarrased occupant, who had 'acquired' a personal locator beacon from a fishing boat, thinking it was an easily disposable piece of electronic equipment, had some explaining to do to the policemen who called on precise directions from the helicopter and found the device in an upstairs wardrobe. All concerned in the official side of this episode took it in good part as a proof of the efficiency of the system.

Rescue helicopter ranges and payloads gradually built up, first with the fitting of turboshaft (Gnôme) engines into the RAF's Whirlwinds making them 'Mark 10s'. The Navy's Whirlwinds were similarly up-powered either by conversion or new-build replacement and the equivalent of the RAF's Mark 10 became the HAS-7.

In March 1954 a new Sikorsky helicopter, the S-58, first flew. Six years later the Royal Navy took delivery of its first Westland-built version, named the Wessex. This helicopter type was to be the basic vehicle for many changes and improvements, not least in the search and rescue world. The Royal Navy's first Wessex aircraft with 1,100 hp Napier Gazelle turboshaft engines in place of the Americans' original piston Wright R-1820-84s were the first electronic helicopters with power control and automatic flight systems

A Mark II Nimrod with refuelling probe *(British Aerospace)*.

A Mark 10 Gnôme-engined Whirlwind of 'C' Flight, 22 Squadron, RAF Valley, exercising with the Holyhead lifeboat. The Mark 10 Whirlwind, mainstay of the RAF rescue flights for many years, was powered by a single Bristol Siddeley (later Rolls-Royce) 1,050 shaft horsepower Gnôme. It had a loaded weight of 8,000 lb and could lift four or five survivors during rescue operations according to fuel state. It had a cruising speed of 104 mph and normally operated on a fifty-mile radius over the sea.

making all-weather, night-and-day flying a practical proposition.

The Royal Navy's prime requirement for this sort of helicopter flying was in the realm of submarine hunting; for the 'dunking' of sonar buoys both night and day and in all weathers. Nevertheless the facility was obviously going to have an important bearing on search and rescue techniques too.

Night, and low-visibility flying in earlier types of helicopter had been difficult and usually discouraged if not actually forbidden. The essential problem had always been the necessity for the pilot to have a visual reference while hovering, while his aeroplane's lack of forward progress through the air nullified most of the standard flying instruments.

The first total darkness helicopter rescue on record took place in 1963 when a Sea Vixen from HMS *Ark Royal* ditched in the Gulf of Aden and the pilot was picked up by the ship's duty SAR Wessex flown by Lieutenant, later

The Burndept 'SARBE' beacon.

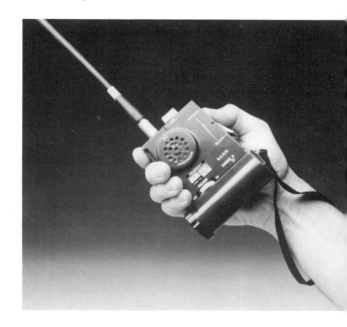

The twin-rotor Bristol Belvedere helicopters had limited success in the RAF service and were never officially tasked for rescue work. It was not normally fitted with winch-gear but around Christmas 1962 one was called out, together with a Shackleton to help the crew of an RAF launch in distress off the South Malayan coast. Several members of the RAF launch crew were lifted into the Belvedere by 'pussers' block-and-tackle gear. The damaged launch, which had hit an underwater obstruction, with the remainder of its crew was later towed into safe harbour on Singapore Island by another RAF rescue pinnace. This incident perhaps created a record in which an RAF rescue launch crew was rescued by an RAF helicopter.

Commander, Victor Sirett. He in fact used an instrument connected to the cable of his sonar buoy to achieve an accurate hover on a night whose luminosity he likened to that of part of the intimate anatomy of a witch.

Helicopter rescues at night and in poor visibility had, of course, been carried out before, perhaps with some rule-bending, perhaps with the benison of some visual reference being provided by street lights, car headlamps or shafts of moonlight; but it was the Navy's requirement for an automatic flying control system, providing for an accurate hover of about 40 ft altitude while dunking a sonar buoy, that made for the real breakthrough.

Until the 1960s too helicopter pilots had about as much liking for mountains as their fixed-wing counterparts, especially in the days of the piston-engined aircraft which did not respond well to sixty-knot vertical downdraughts on the lee sides of ridges in strong winds. Some gallant and successful rescue operations were carried out in the mountains — particularly in Snowdonia 'hard by' No 22 Squadron's 'C' Flight at Valley — but it was the advent of the Mark 10 Gnôme-engined Whirlwind which made this sort of work practicable.

As the RAF's Mark 10 Whirlwinds came into service advice was sought from, and freely given by, the French Armée de L'Air which had acquired much experience during the campaigns in Algeria and Indo-China (later Vietnam). During a series of interchange visits helicopter mountain rescue techniques were adopted by the RAF which stand to the present day.

Helicoptering in mountains remains hazardous even with the best of modern equipment, particularly for the winchmen. Apart from the down-draughting and up-draughting there is the constant hazard of sudden visibility loss through clouds suddenly drifting into peaks and ridges. Obviously any loss of power at a critical moment means catastrophe for all concerned. The later replacement of the still single-engined Whirlwind Mark 10s by twin-engined Wessex and by Sea Kings in the RAF Rescue Flights thus brought much comfort to the SAR crews involved in mountain work.

An early problem in the mountains was that the Whirlwind winch cables only provided for a hover of a maximum of 50 ft, better 30 ft. Various expedients were used, including the attachment of climbers' ropes to the winch cables, later extension 'straps' made of webbing.

The then Flight Sergeant (later Flight Lieutenant) John Donnelly of 22 Squadron won the first of two Air Force Medals on 19 May 1974 after tying 200 ft of climbing rope to his aircraft's winch cable and having himself lowered and 'pendulum-swung' under an overhang to rescue an injured climber.

A Wessex HAR 2 of 'C' Flight, 22 Squadron, RAF Valley, in one of its 'hunting grounds' near the Plas-Y-Brenin Mountaineering Centre in North Wales. The HAR 2 Wessex has twin-coupled 1,350 shp Gnômes, a loaded weight of 13,500 lb and a maximum sea level speed of 132 mph *(Derek Mayes)*.

Even if direct rescue by winching or by ground level hovering is not possible helicopters can often play an absolutely vital role in mountain rescue by taking ground teams up to the nearest feasible point and then taking casualties to hospital fast. The latter ability is often of major importance when mountain casualties are suffering from cold and exposure — these days officially called 'hypothermia'.

As rescue helicopters were developed and improved, winching heights were extended — to about 200 ft in the case of the Sea King and 300 ft in the case of the latest versions of the SAR Wessex. When the Sea King was first introduced into RAF service as an SAR helicopter some doubts were expressed about its capability in the mountains, partly because of the hefty downdraught needed to keep ten tons of aeroplane in the hover; but the doubts have been disproved by events.

By the turn of the 1960s/70s decade a structure had been established consisting of a

chain of RAF Mark 10 Whirlwind SAR Flights of 22 and 202 Squadron around the coasts of the UK which could give aid not only to Service aircrews in trouble but also to many civilians. This chain was supported by the Navy's rescue helicopters both ashore and on board ships. There was a well-organised back-up of Maritime Reconnaissance Shackletons. Liaison with the Coastguard, the police, the RNLI and the many volunteer mountain rescue teams was growing apace.

By this time two essential Rescue Co-ordination Centres had been established, one at Pitreavie Castle, near Edinburgh, the other at Mount Wyse, Plymouth. Both were located hard alongside existing Royal Navy RAF liaison organisations. Responsibility for the co-ordination of rescue services could then neatly be divided by a line running from mid-Wales to the Wash.

By late 1969 the Fleet Air Arm had taken delivery of the first of its large and expanding fleet of Sea King helicopters — the Westland-

John Donnelly (at the time of picture holding the rank of Master Air Loadmaster) — a pioneer of mountain rescue techniques among RAF winchmen. *(Derek Booth)*.

built versions of the basic Sikorsky S-61 'shape'. To the Navy these aeroplanes primarily represented an advance in submarine hunter-killer techniques but they also provided for massive extensions of SAR work and techniques. Sea Kings had a radius of action of 200 miles; they could fly and *hover* in nil-visibility and they had a survivor payload of up to twelve adults.

During this period discussion was going on — and indeed is still going on — over whether the responsibility for civilian rescue by helicopter or fixed-wing aircraft should be that of the Armed Forces, or whether in peacetime, it should be that of the Coastguard or the RNLI. An opportunity for an experiment in the latter sort of arrangement arose in 1969 when, because of yet another crisis in the Middle East, the RAF helicopter rescue flight based at Manston had to depart hurriedly.

After some local outcry that 'cover' over

the particularly accident-prone corner of the English Channel and the North Sea had been withdrawn a contract was arranged between HM Coastguard and Bristow Helicopters for the provision of a fleet of 'Series 3' Whirlwinds (civilian equivalents of the RAF's Mark 10s) with competent SAR crews. During its three-year existence this little organisation acquitted itself with much honour, flying 700 rescue sorties and contributing to the preservation of 150 lives. In 1974 'E' Flight of No 22 Squadron moved back into Manston, however, bringing with it the first of the RAF's twin-engined Wessex HAR 5s which were coming into service as well as the Sea Kings to replace the Mark 10 Whirlwinds.

Many more significant advances in the 'state of the art' of search and rescue were made in the 1970s. During this period the whole structure of maritime life in the North Sea was changing. Oil had been discovered, and at about the same time the Scottish fishing fleets were having to venture further and further offshore into perilous waters to meet international competition.

Curiously it was also a period when several overseas nations, including Norway, West Germany and Belgium, were buying Westland Sea Kings specifically for SAR purposes and under a package deal having their crews trained by the Royal Navy at Culdrose. Meanwhile the British nation had to rely on its fleets of single-engined Whirlwinds for its own SAR service.

Some well justified political and press lobbying was applied and as an interim measure another direct Coastguard contract was arranged in 1971 under which the then British European Airways Helicopter company undertook to provide at least one of its Sikorsky S61N passenger helicopters, based at Aberdeen, for the oil rig traffic, to be made available for rescue at a maximum of one hour's notice.

The company recruited a small team of experienced ex-Navy and ex-RAF helicopter rescue experts as crewmen, taught its pilots the rudiments of the techniques required, and bought a set of Lucas Aerospace detachable winches which could be fitted to any of their oil rig passenger 'cabs' in about ten minutes flat. The BEAH American-built S-61s were, of course, civilian equivalents of the Westland Sea Kings which the Royal Navy owned but which could not make available exclusively for rescue because of anti-submarine warfare training commitments.

This Department of Trade/Coastguard/ British European Airways Helicopters deal, like so many other *ad hoc* arrangements of its kind, was highly successful. Among other things it was unique in providing a helicopter-borne medical service, sometimes a helicopter-borne intensive-care unit, because of the special interest in it taken by Dr David Proctor, then head of the accident and casualty service of the Aberdeen Group of hospitals. Dr Proctor flew on eighteen missions himself, many of them to trawlers on board which a crew member had been seriously injured in a typical accident with winchgear or wire rope.

In December 1977 the efficiency of the organisation was dramatically illustrated when a modern Aberdeen trawler, the *Elinor Viking*, struck the notorious Ve Skerries reef five miles north-west of Papa Stour on the northernmost edge of the Shetland archipelago. This is a dreadful place which has taken many mariners' lives. The stand-by BEAH S-61N *(G-ATBJ)* at Sumburgh Airport, Shetland, was airborne within twenty minutes of a Mayday being received from the *Elinor Viking*. (By 1977 the BEAH rescue contract had been extended from Aberdeen to Shetland with the northward march of the oil rigs.)

The crew consisted of Captain George Bain (First Pilot), Captain Campbell Bosanquet (Second Pilot), Mr Brian Johnstone (winch operator) and Captain Alisdair Campbell, a line pilot who had jumped aboard as voluntary winchman.

In appalling weather conditions they found the *Elinor Viking* in their landing lights lying on her side across the rocks, the last part of the search being directed by Mr Johnstone who could smell diesel oil out of the open cabin door. A Nimrod helped them by homing on to one of their Sarbe locator beacons and dropping flares. After eighty minutes' continuous hovering and twelve descents on the winch wire by Captain Campbell all eight aboard, including the

A British Airways Helicopters S-61 operating under the Coastguard rescue contract from Sumburgh, Shetland, attempting to save survivors from a 748 crash *(Daily Mail)*.

Skipper, Alex Flett, were safely lifted. Minutes after Skipper Flett was brought up the ship disintegrated.

Some years earlier two other maritime disasters had, however, led to some profound re-thinking about the whole subject of helicopter rescue and the requirement for larger multi-engined aircraft to be on call.

On 16 January 1974 a 480-ton Danish coaster, the *Merc Enterprise* with nineteen aboard, including three women, capsized south of Plymouth in storm force winds and 30-foot seas. A maximum effort was launched from RNAS Culdrose employing Sea Kings of the Royal Navy and of the West German Navy whose crews were undergoing training there as part of the package sales deal.

In the event eleven of the nineteen were saved, seven of them by the Sea Kings, the remaining four in a particularly gallant effort by crewmen from a Russian trawler. The operation called for many hours of hovering at low altitude in dense salt-laden spray which was ingested into the helicopter engines with the near loss of two of them. Much was learned from that aspect of the rescue and remedial steps taken which have probably preserved many aircrew lives, particularly during the subsequent Falklands War. Certainly no lesser type of helicopter than the Sea King could have coped with the conditions.

Almost exactly a year later the 1,000-ton British coaster *Lovat* ran into trouble in a south-westerly gale off Land's End. Her cargo of fine coal shifted and her Master, Captain Leslie Beeson, sent out a Mayday early in the morning of Saturday 25 January 1975.

The nearest 'declared' helicopter rescue facility consisted of a stand-by Whirlwind at RNAS Culdrose which was on fifteen minutes' notice to scramble during daylight hours. This aircraft lifted off at 07:43 hours, a fourteen-minute delay from first light being

An artist's impression of the *Merc Enterprise* rescue *(RN)*.

caused by some radio communication problems.

The *Lovat* was 25 miles south of Land's End and the Whirlwind only had the capability of lifting three survivors out of a known ship's company of thirteen while still having enough fuel to return to land. Nevertheless it set off and in spite of it being a Saturday 'stand-down' morning and there being no formal commitment for it, immediate steps were taken at Culdrose to get a Sea King airborne. One of these aircraft, technically the property of the Pakistan Navy under the sales package arrangement, lifted off ninety minutes after the alarm with a full Royal Navy crew aboard.

In the meantime the Whirlwind crew had run into trouble. Leading Naval Aircrewman/Diver Peter Gibbs had gone down on the wire to a life raft with five men and a boy aboard, the last already dead. Peter Gibbs was pushed under the water by the first man he tried to help into the strop and was whipped up and then lowered again by his fellow Aircrewman Paul Mansell who was operating the winchgear.

The Whirlwind then lurched in turbulence and the winch wire cut across Peter Gibbs throat so that Paul Mansell had no option but to activate the explosive charge cable cutter. The Whirlwind had by then reached the limit of its fuel endurance and had to leave Peter Gibbs in the life raft with four remaining survivors.

When the Sea King, 'Papa One' arrived overhead Gibbs was able to help two living survivors into the strop and assist in the recovery of bodies, one being that of a young sailor who had succumbed to hypothermia in spite of his having clasped him in his arms in an effort to preserve life. Peter Gibbs was later awarded the Queen's Gallantry Medal.

Considerable debate followed this tragedy, some in the lobbies of the House of Commons, some in the columns of *The Times* and *The Guardian*, raising the question of why the British nation should not be able to provide Sea Kings for rescue purposes at short notice when it had the aircraft and probably had more expertise in the handling of them than any other European nation.

Several events followed although it was never established whether they were coincidental or *because* of the *Lovat* affair. It

Peter Gibbs, QGM, after the *Lovat* tragedy *(RN)*.

is fairly obvious however, that at least it acted as a catalyst to speed up some actions which may have already have been under consideration.

The first step was an announcement on 1 April 1975 that a new Department of Trade (Coastguard) arrangement with the Navy would provide for Sea Kings to be available for rescue work from Culdrose and from Prestwick in Scotland at a maximum of two hours notice. A substantial number of Sea Kings were, and still are, normally based at Culdrose for training. Others are often ashore there from ships undergoing re-fits. The Prestwick Sea Kings are the equipment of No 819 NAS, the only front-line Naval Air Squadron permanently ashore with the primary role of exercising with Clyde-based submarines.

In the years to come this arrangement was to lead to many dramatic and successful rescue operations. The 'dedicated' Fleet Air Arm SAR Flights at Lee-on-Solent and at

A Mark 2 HAS (anti-submarine) Sea King from RNAS Culdrose. The special assets possessed by Sea Kings as 'rescuers' include the Newmark Automatic Flying Control System which provides for a hands-off hover at approximately 40 ft above smooth sea or flat ground level — originally devised to facilitate sonar dunking — and an Auxiliary Hover Trim lever mounted above the main door by which a winch operator can 'fly' the aircraft over the last few feet of adjustment when picking up a survivor. The Royal Air Force Mark 3 HAR Sea Kings (see next picture) are also equipped with the TANS (Tactical Air Navigation System) aid which is often of great value in finding a precise position at night or in bad visibility *(Rolls-Royce)*.

Culdrose, equipped with Wessex, remained available to help in civilian rescue operations — the latter aircraft playing a particularly prominent part in the saving of life during the Fastnet yacht race tragedy of August 1979.

During the same mid-1970s period the RAF's long-standing bid for a fleet of Sea King HAR 3s — special versions of the type designed exclusively for rescue work — was accepted. The purchase of fifteen of them at a price of about £20 million was authorised and the first were in service by 1979. By that time another replacement programme substituting twin-engined versions of the Wessex for some of the Whirlwinds was also under way.

The whole re-equipment programme was accompanied by a re-organisation which put all the Sea Kings into 202 Squadron, the remaining Whirlwinds, being progressively replaced by Wessex, into 22 Squadron. This made for commonsense on both the engineering and administrative sides and an SAR headquarters was established roughly in the middle of the country at Finningley, South Yorkshire, comprising a Wing and two Squadron HQs and workshop facilities which could handle anything up to major overhauls.

By the beginning of the 1980s Britain had a search and rescue organisation which is rightly claimed to be the best in the world in relation to the sea area, coastline length and mountain areas covered. There have been some minor changes since 1980, though.

The rescue helicopter locations, starting in the extreme north and working in a clockwise direction are as follows.

In the major oilfields such as the Forties and the Brent there are 'self-help' units, permanently located on offshore platforms consisting of civilian aircraft which can be quickly adapted to the rescue role with a back-up of doctors and other medical facilities. These aircraft can divert to incidents unrelated to the oil industry if necessary.

At least one 'dedicated' S-61N helicopter is located at Sumburgh Airport, Shetland. This facility, still part of a direct Coastguard contract, was originally provided by British Airways Helicopters, but was taken over by Bristow in December, 1983 when the former company concentrated its oilfield activities on Aberdeen with long-range Chinooks as its 'passenger cabs'.

At least two Sea Kings of 202 Squadron are based at Lossiemouth on the Moray Firth. There are Wessex of 22 Squadron at Leuchars, Fifeshire; Sea Kings at Boulmer, Northumberland; Wessex at Leconfield, Yorkshire; Sea Kings at Coltishall, Norfolk; and Wessex at Manston, Kent.

Moving along the south coast there are the Navy's Wessex at Lee-on-Solent and at Culdrose plus the Sea King back-up mentioned above. The RAF has a Wessex Flight at Chivenor, north Devon; Sea Kings at Brawdy, Pembrokeshire; and Wessex at Valley, Anglesey. The west of Scotland is covered by the 819 Naval Air Squadron Sea Kings at Prestwick. The fixed-wing SAR element is provided by Nimrods based at Kinloss, Morayshire and St Mawgan, Cornwall, each of the four squadrons taking it in weekly turns to provide one aircraft on quick reaction stand-by loaded with an extra set of Lindholme Gear.

That is by no means the whole of it.

At Woodbridge in Suffolk there is a remarkable unit of the United States Air Force, a detachment of the 67th Aerospace Rescue and Recovery Squadron. It is equipped with Sikorsky HH-53C 'Super Jolly Green Giant' helicopters and C-130 (Hercules) tankers. Their helicopters are among the only ones of their kind in the Western world capable of in-flight refuelling, and thereby have unlimited range. They are

One of the special ways in which a helicopter can save life is that of getting casualties suffering from cold ('hypothermia') into warm conditions quickly. It is only in relatively recent years that the danger of cold has been fully assessed in relation to that of drowning in distress situations at sea. Cold has a 'sneaky' effect in that a survivor may feel quite comfortable once his own body temperature descends to that of the outside air or water and he may then give up fighting for life. This effect is dramatically illustrated in the picture above, taken by a Royal Navy rescue helicopter crewman during the Fastnet yacht race disaster. The yachtsman shown, a highly experienced sailor, is well clad with his life jacket properly inflated and he shows no signs of distress in his posture nor facial expression. He had in fact, been dead for several hours before the helicopter found him. *(Leading Naval Aircrewman Photographer Steven Pratt, RN).*

also armed and armoured. The squadron's role is a world-wide one and has some connections with the possible necessary recovery of space vehicles.

This unit is ready, willing and indeed anxious, to assist in UK rescue operations but its huge aircraft necessarily take a long time to 'wind-up' for a scramble — about ninety minutes at best. For that reason they cannot often 'compete' with the quick reaction times of the RAF's and the Navy's Wessex and Sea Kings. Nevertheless they have contributed, often without public recognition, in such episodes as the West Country blizzards of 1978, the search for possible survivors of the Air India Jumbo and the fairly recent loss of a

trawler 'outwith' the range even of Sea Kings off the north-west of Scotland.

This writer feels that inevitably 'their day will come' and he would welcome it, having met some of the very staunch characters who fly and maintain these extraordinary rotary-wing aeroplanes and their accompanying C-130 tankers, some of the latter being female and also very staunch.

In-flight refuelling in a helicopter remains one of the most hazardous operations open to any airman. One only has to visualise the maximum forward speed of a helicopter of about 130 knots and the minimum stalling speed of a heavily loaded C-130 tanker to imagine the stresses involved for all

A Sikorsky HH-53C 'Super Jolly Green Giant' of the 67th Aerospace Rescue and Recovery Squadron, USAF, at Woodbridge, Suffolk. Maximum weight 42,000 lb; 600 miles range *without* in-flight refuelling *(USAF)*.

concerned. The United States Air Force regularly practises this technique at altitudes of about 1,000 ft and in war would have to carry it out at tree-top height. It is *not* a popular sport within the USAF.

At RAF Valley, Anglesey, in addition to 'C' Flight of 22 Squadron there are the Wessex helicopters of the Search and Rescue Training Unit (SARTU). In the hands of instructors these aircraft can often make a major contribution to a rescue operation in an area where both sailors and mountaineers find themselves in trouble fairly frequently.

Helicopters based on board ships of the Royal Navy and the Royal Fleet Auxiliary can often be in the right place at the right time to help. The Navy's present fleet of aircraft carriers, HMSs *Invincible, Illustrious and Ark Royal,* all carry Sea Kings, so do several of the RFA's bigger supply ships. The replacement of the Navy's small anti-submarine Wasp helicopters in medium-sized ships such as destroyers and frigates, by Lynxes, has brought about a further rescue potential. The Lynx is quite capable of rescue by winch and has proved itself in this role on several occasions. The Wasps 'could do it' — but only just.

Within the RAF No 72 Squadron, equipped with Wessex at Aldergrove in Northern Ireland, is, of course, primarily a support unit concerned with the movement of troops and supplies in this 'war zone' but it

can, and does, take on rescue tasks, a fairly recent one involving a Sealink ferry which took fire off the Antrim coast. Very few television viewers really noticed that the rescue helicopters shown on film were dark blue Royal Navy Sea Kings from Prestwick and grey-painted Wessex of 72 Squadron from Aldergrove. Slightly to the chagrin of the RAF's SAR Wing no yellow Wessex nor Sea Kings got there in time.

Apart from the self-help arrangements paid for by the oil companies a great many helicopters are always available in a crisis from Dyce Airport, Aberdeen. Several participated in a recent oil rig evacuation task without much public recognition.

Perhaps the most important extension of the British Search and Rescue organisation during the 1970s and 1980s, however, concerned the links established with neighbouring countries. The 'package deals' over the Sea Kings established by Westland and the Royal Navy had something to do with this. Out of them emerged particularly close liaison arrangements across the North Sea with the links between the RAF and the Royal Norwegian Air Force.

On several occasions it has made sense for RAF and civilian rescue helicopters based in northern Scotland to collect casualties from an oil rig in the middle of the North Sea in westerly gale conditions to proceed under a tail wind to Stavanger or thereabouts. Equally it has sometimes made sense for Scandinavian-based helicopters to proceed to Scottish bases with their casualties in easterly or north-easterly 'blows'. The classic example of Anglo-Norwegian rescue co-operation in the case of the Alexander Kielland oil rig disaster of March 1980 will be described in more detail later.

On the other side of the country some very important relationships have been established with the government of the Irish Republic. For a number of sound reasons these have been 'under-publicised'. Under international agreements the Irish government has responsibilities for safety and for life-saving over a vast area of hostile ocean — a large slice of the eastern half of the Atlantic in fact sometimes called the Shannon sea area. It has always done its best to meet these obligations within its capabilities as a small country.

An Army Air Corps Sioux. These little aircraft carried out hundreds of casualty evacuation tasks in such 'theatres of war' as Borneo and Northern Ireland *(Army Air Corps)*.

The existing, rather informal, and rightly under-publicised arrangements provide for rescue helicopters of the Royal Navy and the Royal Air Force to overfly Irish airspace and to refuel at Irish bases, even though they are strictly speaking 'military aircraft'. The same sort of overflying arrangement applies to RAF Nimrods on SAR missions. There has never been any problem about this sort of arrangement and many, many lives have been saved as a result of it.

In addition the Irish Air Corps has built up a small, but most efficient, fleet of rescue helicopters whose work seldom gets much recognition. Their air and ground crews have close relationships with their counterparts at the Royal Navy and RAF Sea King bases at Culdrose and Brawdy. On many occasions they have worked together to save lives. In this context it might be important to reiterate that the lifeboat service in the Irish Republic is operated by the *Royal* National Lifeboat Institution. There are, in fact, no silly political barriers when it comes to a rescue job by helicopter or lifeboat, or Nimrod, or any other suitable machine of man's making.

The British Army Air Corps, founded in the late 1950s out of an amalgam of the Royal Artillery Air Observation Post squadrons, the Glider Pilot Regiment and other elements of the wartime Airborne Forces, is now probably the biggest 'user' of helicopters among the three Armed Forces in this country.

Army helicopters have never been 'dedicated' to the search and rescue role. Nevertheless their crews have been instrumental in the saving and preservation of hundreds, perhaps thousands of human lives. Most of the Army's life-saving role by helicopter and sometimes by fixed-wing aircraft has been concerned with casualty evacuation in such 'minor war' theatres as Aden, Borneo, Cyprus and right up to the present day, Northern Ireland.

Army pilots and crewmen have plucked wounded soldiers out of jungles and deserts; have extracted pregnant women from similar places and sometimes helped to deliver their babies en route. Some British Army helicopters have carried out 'air-sea' rescues from stormy Northern Ireland lakes and estuaries and from the extensive waters surrounding Hong Kong over which many venture in search of freedom.

The Army Air Corps does not make much fuss about its secondary, or perhaps tertiary, role of life-saving. Its air and ground crews are just pleased to do what they can when the occasion arises. Against this background some more stories can now be told of individual rescue operations.

Chapter Six
Some notable recent rescues

The incidents described in detail in this chapter must, of course, only be regarded as a cross-section of several thousand which have been recorded since the helicopter/maritime reconnaissance aircraft rescue structure was established in Britain more than thirty years ago. They have been selected to illustrate the special qualities of the current SAR organisation's technical equipment and the courage and devotion to duty so often called for from all concerned, both in the air and on the ground.

To the time of writing the largest and most complex rescue operation, involving both fixed and rotary winged aircraft, surface ships, and four nations, occurred at the end of March 1980 when the 'accommodation' oil rig, *Alexander L. Kielland*, capsized in the middle of the North Sea; 170 nautical miles east by south of Aberdeen, 150 nm south-west of Lista in southern Norway and 165 nm west of Bovbjerg in Denmark. The final count recorded 123 lives lost and 89 saved.

Nineteen helicopters of the Royal Air Force, the Royal Norwegian Air Force and of a Norwegian civil company (Helikopter Service AS), plus seven large fixed-wing MR aircraft (six RAF Nimrods and a Norwegian Orion) participated, as well as Danish and West German Sea Kings. Eighty surface vessels also took part.

A great many words have already been written and printed about this disaster which became a copybook example of co-operation between aircraft and surface vessels, and between nations.

The first Mayday call went out at 18:29 hours on 27 March 1980. On the British side of the North Sea a Sea King of 'A' Flight 202 Squadron, RAF, was scrambled and lifted off from Boulmer, Northumberland, ten minutes later, using callsign 'Rescue 31' and crewed by Flight Lieutenant Robert Neville (1st Pilot

and Captain), Flight Lieutenant Michael Lakey (Second Pilot, or 'P2'), Flight Sergeant (later Flight Lieutenant) John Moody as navigator and winch operator and Flight Sergeant Michael Yarwood as winchman. This aircraft reached the designated search area by 20:30 hours and ninety minutes later saw a life raft with ten people aboard. — Flight Sergeant Yarwood went down on the winch and had to unhook himself and drop into the sea twice before being able to board the life raft. The survivors aboard it were winched up into the Sea King and dropped on to the nearest oil rig platform. Flight Lieutenants Neville and Lakey then climbed rapidly to 2,000 ft to clear the fog which was gathering to add to the hazards of sixty-knot winds with thirty-foot waves which had brought about the disaster in the first place.

They then picked up a characteristic signal from an automatic locator beacon and descended on to it. They saw a lifeboat with 26 people aboard. Flight Sergeant Yarwood descended again on the winch wire — after some altercation with his Captain as to his physical fitness resulting from his previous immersions. He went down, had a look at the situation in the lifeboat, was winched up again, and told Flight Lieutenant Neville that the survivors were not in a critical condition and the the most constructive course of action would be to record the position and guide surface vessels to it. This was duly done.

Meanwhile SAR Sea Kings from No 330 Squadron, Royal Norwegian Air Force, winched up a total of 43 survivors from two lifeboats. One of them, using callsign 'Viking 50', picked up thirty men, but at one stage its winch wire became entangled around one of the boats and had to be cut. Another Norwegian Sea King had to land on a rig for rapid repairs to its defective winch gear.

Apart from the initial 'search' phase the

work done by the Kinloss Nimrods and the Orion of 333 Squadron, Royal Norwegian Air Force, became absolutely critical in the later control and co-ordination aspects of the whole operation. A great many helicopters were trying to help in very bad visibility conditions and the Nimrod Captains found themselves taking on the role of airborne traffic controllers with a prime task of preventing mid-air collisions. There was in fact one 'near miss' of about 70 ft separation, only averted by the vigilance and quick reaction of a Nimrod crew plus excellent radio communications.

One message recorded concerned a conversation between the young Flight Lieutenant Captain of a Nimrod and a Very Senior Officer on the lines of: 'Will you please call off some of your helicopters *Sir* or we shall have another disaster on our hands'.

Statistics gathered later showed that 387 hours 50 minutes' flying time was put in by aircraft of all types during the rescue operation, 319 of them by helicopter.

The essential co-ordination from the ground was the prime responsibility of the Norwegian control centres at Stavanger in the south and at Bodo in the north; but the British centres at Pitreavie and Aberdeen did everything they could to help. In the inevitable long 'inquests' into the disaster no one could fault the acts and spirit of co-operation shown by all concerned that night. Numerous British and Norwegian decorations were deservedly bestowed upon many concerned.

One recipient was Flight Lieutenant Michael Lakey who earned the Guild of Air Pilots and Air Navigators Prince Philip Bravery Award for the part he played as P2 of 'Rescue 31'. He went down to London for the presentation ceremony and twenty minutes after getting back to his new base at Lossiemouth he was called out as P1 of the second stand-by Sea King to assist a ship in distress.

This was the Swedish container vessel *Finneagle* with sixty tons of dangerous chemicals in its cargo which had caught fire in storm force winds about sixty miles north-west of the Orkneys. It was the night of 1 October 1980. There were 22 people on board including some women and children.

The first stand-by Sea King from Lossiemouth had been scrambled under callsign 'Rescue 37' and had the ship in sight by 22:30 hours. Radio messages had been received that the crew and passengers were mustered on the foredeck but were having difficulty in breathing because of noxious fumes.

A British Airways winch-equipped S-61N had also been scrambled from Sumburgh, Shetland under the Department of Transport/Coastguard contract arrangement.

Both these aircraft were encountering extreme difficulties because of the height of the flames from burning deck cargo and the movement of the ship's masts and aerials. Attempts were made by the ship's crew to cut down the latter but both 'Rescue 37' and 'Rescue 17' (the BAH S-61) had to break off the task having reached the limit of their fuel endurance, and return to Kirkwall in Orkney.

Flight Lieutenant Lakey's 'Rescue 38', which had a doctor on board, was able to go straight into action, however, and the crew eventually winched to safety all on board the *Finneagle*. To do this they used the by then well-established Hi-line procedure, believed to have been originally developed by Norwegian helicopter rescue crews. The technique involves the helicopter first making a fairly high pass over a stricken ship or yacht and dropping a 100-ft weighted line vertically to the deck. The theory is that someone on the vessel — and all ship's crews and many yachtsmen are now familiar with the technique — should take hold of the line, but resist the sailor's instinct to make it fast to something. (Helicopter crews do NOT like being tied to ships.)

The system provides for a descending winchman and ascending survivors to be 'steered' through rigging, masts and other obstructions. It also provides the helicopter pilot with a clear view of what is going on and releases him from total dependence on the intercom 'patter' from the winch operator.

The ship or yacht should endeavour to steer and make headway at about 20 degrees to starboard of the true wind direction to enable the helicopter to fly dead into wind while hovering. This procedure (obviously not alway possible) also helps the pilot to keep the ship in view from his right hand seat. (Unlike

The crew of the 202 Squadron Sea King who saved 36 lives during the *Alexander Kielland* disaster. Standing: Flight Sergeant Mike Yarwood. Kneeling left to right: Flight Lieutenant Bob Neville, Flight Sergeant (later Flight Lieutenant) Bob Moody and Flight Lieutenant Mike Lakey who later figured in the *Finneagle* rescue *(Newcastle Chronicle)*.

fixed-wing aircraft, the command position in a helicopter is always on the right.) If a ship's crew is competent and sufficiently fit it may not be necessary for the helicopter winchman to go down at all, but sometimes he has to take his chance among gyrating masts and wires first in order to take charge of the procedure.

There was obviously the danger of a major explosion on the *Finneagle* at any time and the ship was quickly dubbed 'the floating bomb' in newspaper headlines. It took forty minutes of hovering in conditions of extreme turbulence to complete the uplift of the 22 on board. At one point there was a gout of flame

from the deck leading to a quick cry of 'Up' from Flight Lieutenant Thomas Campbell, the winch operator and an equally rapid reaction on the collective pitch lever by Michael Lakey.

During the first lift the helicopter crew saw that two women, each clutching a child, had put themselves in the strop together. They were all four safely gathered in. None of the survivors sustained serious injury.

A senior officer of the Coastguard later commented publicly: 'The rescue by Michael Lakey and his crew in Rescue 38 was the most outstanding in my experience.

'There was every possibility of the vessel

All that was visible of the *Alexander Kielland* by daybreak *(Associated Press)*.

exploding at any moment during the long winching operation in appalling storm conditions and a raging fire.'

During the next twelve hours the tug *Carabic* fought and controlled the fire and took the *Finneagle* in tow to Lerwick where the cargo was made safe.

Flight Lieutenant Lakey was awarded the George Medal: Flight Lieutenant Campbell the Air Force Cross; Sergeant Richard Bragg (the winchman) the Air Force Medal; and Flight Lieutenant David Simpson (P2) the Queen's Commendation for Service in the Air. Squadron Leader Hamish Grant, the Senior Medical Officer at RAF Lossiemouth, who had joined the crew voluntarily, also received a Queen's Commendation.

On 18 November 1980 a Sea King of 'C' Flight 202 Squadron was scrambled from Coltishall following a report that two USAF A-10 Thunderbolts had collided while approaching a weapons range off the Norfolk coast. One pilot had ejected safely over land; the other, Lieutenant-Colonel William Olsen, had attempted to reach his base at Bentwaters in Suffolk by flying his damaged aircraft over the sea, thus avoiding built-up areas and risk of injury to people on the ground. A few miles off the Norfolk coast, near the village of Winterton, his aircraft finally went out of control and he too had to eject.

For the crew of the Coltishall Sea King it looked like a routine job. 'Armed Forces' rescues of this type, accounting for about ten per cent of the SAR helicopters' 'trade', seldom present serious problems because all concerned are well equipped and well trained for survival. The weather conditions were rough, but reasonable with a 40-to 45-knot wind and 15-ft waves.

The Coltishall Sea King homed on to Colonel Olsen's locator beacon without difficulty but the crew saw that his parachute was still partially deployed and attached to him, and that he was being dragged through the waves by it in corkscrew fashion. Two of the RAF's most experienced winchmen, Master Air Electronics Operator John Reeson, GM (who had won his decoration fifteen years earlier for his part in a gas rig rescue) and Master Air Loadmaster David Bullock, were at the back end of the Sea King.

Dave Bullock went down on the wire, seized hold of Colonel Olsen's legs and was dragged behind him, also in corkscrew fashion. The rest of the Sea King crew watched helplessly as the two men in the water seemed to become inextricably entangled in the parachute cords.

Eventually, and for the first and only time on record, a helicopter winch wire, with a breaking strain of 3,700 lb, parted; under the combined forces of a parachute half-full of sea water driven by a 40-knot wind and an aircraft capable of supporting ten tons of its all-up weight in the air.

The resulting tragedy was a deeply poignant one for all concerned, especially for John Reeson who, with all his experience and knowledge, was unable to do a thing to help his friend Dave Bullock. The sea state was, of course, far too rough for the Sea King to attempt a 'water-alighting', which this type of helicopter can sometimes achieve in fair weather conditions.

There were even more poignant moments to come. The fighter aircraft involved were American and the 67th Aerospace Rescue and Recovery Squadron at Woodbridge had scrambled one of their 'Super Jolly Green Giants' immediately on receipt of the Mayday signals from the A-10s. Because of factors explained in the previous chapter it took them some time to lift off and reach the scene. The crew of this helicopter included men cross-trained in parachuting, sub-aqua diving, first aid and many other arts. Two crewmen from the Super Jolly Green Giant were in the water alongside Colonel Olsen and David Bullock in a very short time, but not quite quickly enough.

Modifications to the Americans' fighter pilot parachutes were made as a result of this tragedy which was deeply felt throughout the close and small search and rescue world.

It was in fact the first fatal accident involving either a crewman or survivor after thirty years of successful helicopter rescue operations, most of them by the very nature of things being carried out in conditions which airmen dislike most — high winds, bad visibility and close proximity with sea or land. MALM Bullock was subsequently awarded a posthumous George Medal.

There was another tragedy in November 1986 when a Support Wessex on its way to 'medevac' the pregnant wife of a Serviceman crashed into the sea off Cyprus. Among those killed was Master Air Loadmaster Peter Barwell who had won the Air Force Cross for a 1975 rescue off Orkney. An RAF midwife, Flight Lieutenant Fiona Johnstone, and a medical attendant, Corporal Martin Crook, were also killed.

The safety record achieved during the whole history of helicopter rescue, which began with some fairly frail single-engined aircraft, stands as a tribute to the skills and dedication not only of aircrew but of ground or shipboard technicians as well.

During the afternoon of 19 December 1981 the 1,400-ton coaster *Union Star*, new from her builders, reported loss of engine power and impending cargo shift off the Wolf Rock. Receipt of this message by the Coastguard resulted among other things in the mobilisation of a Sea King and its crew at Culdrose under the Royal Navy stand-by arrangements described in the previous chapter. A fully trained and qualified SAR crew consisting of Lieutenant-Commander Russell Smith, USN (on an exchange posting), Lieutenant Stephen Marlow, Sub-Lieutenant Kenneth Doherty and Leading Naval Aircrewman Martin Kennie was summoned by bleeper.

They were all members of No 820 Naval Air Squadron, temporarily shore-based. Their aircraft was 'ranged and spread' fifteen minutes after the alert. By that time the ground crews had also loaded special SAR equipment including a Pye VHF radio for direct communications with the Coastguard and others on the Channel 16 emergency frequency.

The ship was by this time aground off Land's End and it was learned that those on board included a mother with two teenage girls travelling with their stepfather who was the ship's captain. The tragic event which was to ensue became known as 'The Penlee Lifeboat Disaster.' Eight lifeboatmen and eight of the crew of the *Union Star* perished.

In all the welter of words which followed the part played by the Sea King crew was almost submerged, perhaps because their gallant efforts were unsuccessful, perhaps because the aircraft Captain had returned to the United States before the subsequent public inquiries and had to submit written evidence only. Curiously, no gallantry awards were made.

No writer, however much he might be striving for drama, could better the facts and descriptions contained in Lieutenant-Commander Smith's sortie report. It says that during the transit flight from Culdrose to the scene of the disaster a fifty-knot wind was recorded with wave heights on the sea of between 40 and 45 ft. There was heavy rain, poor visibility, low cloud and as darkness descended, no moon.

When they arrived over the stricken ship it was lying beam on to the swell and dragging towards the cliffs. By then the wind was recorded as between 60 and 65 knots gusting to 75-80 knots. At 19:50 hours he and his crew made attempts to carry out normal 'double-lift' rescues with the winchman (initially LACMN Kennie) going down on the wire to try to pluck up one survivor at a time.

They first tried to do this from the starboard quarter of the ship but the combination of the ship's movement with its masts gyrating under wind and wave and the throwing about of the Sea King in the turbulence made it impossible. A second attempt was then made with LACMN Kennie on the wire. He got within fifteen feet of the ship's deck but by then the aircraft was dangerously close to its main mast.

The Sea King crew then made *six* attempts at a Hi-line transfer under the system described above. Their standard 100-ft line was too short because of the height of the *Union Star's* masts so the winchman was lowered on the main cable first with the rope in his hands. Once the rope caught in some

rigging but they managed to recover it. Another time the line dragged across the ship's deck only a few feet from some crew members but no one made any effort to seize it.

At last a member of the ship's crew got hold of the line but the combination of the ship's roll and the aircraft tossing in the turbulence snatched it from his grasp. The aircrew then thought of the expedient of knotting two ropes together but had to abandon this idea because the only spare rope in the aircraft was too thin. (During all of this Sub-Lieutenant Doherty and LACMN Kennie were alternating 'on the wire' and operating the winch gear under the standard cross-training procedure which apply to all at the 'back end' of a rescue helicopter.)

At this stage the wind was recorded at between 65 and 70 knots, gusting to 85 knots. The aircrew could see the *Union Star* drifting even closer to the rocks and they saw the Penlee lifeboatmen making their valiant efforts to get alongside. Even then, Lieutenant-Commander Smith's report said: 'There seemed to no sense of urgency from the ship's crew'.

Yet another Hi-line was dropped but when the weight on the end of it dropped into a wave it snapped in spite of a 250 lb breaking

The wreck of the *Union Star* (RNAS Culdrose).

strain. Two more 'double lift' attempts were made with either Sub-Lieutenant Doherty or LACMN Kennie going down on the wire but both the aircraft and the ship were by then being thrown about so violently that they failed. Seventy-foot high breakers could be seen and the cliff tops disappeared in a haze of flying spray.

The aircrew saw the beginning of the disaster to the Penlee lifeboat as it was picked up on a huge wave, straddled the *Union Star's* hatch covers and then slid back into the sea again. Reluctantly, Commander Smith then had to break off his rescue attempt because in spite of all the power reserves of a Sea King his aircraft was sometimes being blown backwards towards the by now almost invisible cliff tops.

They landed back at Culdrose at 21:35 hours but lifted off again at 22:45 to search for possible survivors at an altitude of about 200 ft. This time, Commander Smith reported, the turbulence was even worse and it was impossible to fly anything approaching an accurate search pattern. They had to return to base.

*   *   *

Among many other things the Falklands War of 1982 was a testing ground for the modern breed of helicopter, especially for the Royal Navy's Sea Kings. They, or perhaps more accurately their air and ground crews, performed many prodigious feats, several of them in the rescue role.

Although it was not until the end of hostilities that a 'dedicated' helicopter rescue unit arrived in the form of a detachment from 202 Squadron, RAF, the Royal Navy's Sea Kings were involved in the saving of many lives during the course of the war. The most dramatic and best recorded incident occurred on 8 June when the Royal Fleet Auxiliary *Sir Galahad* was hit and set on fire at Fitzroy. The casualty list was distressingly high but would have been higher still if it had not been for the work of a number of Sea King crews.

The first in action were Lieutenant John Miller and Petty Officer Aircrewman Alan Ashdown who were in the act of off-loading Rapier anti-aircraft weapons from the ship in their Mark 4 'Commando' Sea King 'VZ' of 846 NAS when the attack came in. They saw it

happening and hovered for a bit out of sight of the enemy behind high ground. They then flew in to lift survivors from the foredeck of *Sir Galahad* and took them ashore five at a time. (To maximise payload the Mk 4 'Commando' Sea Kings were flown in action with one pilot and one aircrewman only. The aircrewmen were qualified as capable of taking over flying controls in emergency.)

The next helicopter to help was a Mark 2 Sea King of 825 Naval Air Squadron captained by the Commanding Officer, Lieutenant-Commander Hugh Clark with Sub-Lieutenant Brian Evans as P2 and Chief Petty Officer David Jackson as aircrewman in the back.

No 825 NAS had been re-commissioned, from a much earlier disbandment, especially for the Falklands War and was equipped with fairly elderly Mk 2 Sea Kings normally used for training at Culdrose. The aircraft had been stripped of their anti-submarine radar and sonar training equipment so that they could act as troop and load carriers. They were flown and maintained by a mixture of Culdrose instructional staff plus a back-up from 814, 819 and 824 Naval Air Squadrons.

Lieutenant-Commander Clark, his crew, and his aeroplane achieved immortality because they were photographed moving in through smoke and flame to lift survivors off the stern of *Sir Galahad*. Hugh Clark's own recollections as told to this author are typically modest. He recalls that he was able to maintain a satisfactory 20-ft altitude hover by using the lettering on the stern of the ship, still visible through the smoke cloud, as a visual reference.

After CPO Jackson had lifted all the survivors who could put themselves into his strop the pilots assisted life rafts loaded with burned and injured Welsh Guardsmen to get ashore by blowing them in the right direction with their rotor downwash.

Three other 825 Squadron Sea Kings also helped. Lieutenants Phil Sheldon and John Boughton were each awarded the Queen's Gallantry Medal for their parts. Lieutenant-Commander Clark was awarded the DSC for 'showing total disregard for his own safety' during the episode. The crew of a Wessex also played a gallant part which went almost unrecognised.

Lieutenant Commander Hugh Clark, CO of 825 Naval Air Squadron during the Falklands operation. He was awarded the Distinguished Service Cross *(RNAS Culdrose)*.

Immediately after the attack on HMS *Coventry* in which nineteen died a Mark 4 Commando Sea King of 846 NAS flown by the CO, Lieutenant-Commander Simon Thornewill, moved in, and its Aircrewman, Chief Petty Officer 'Alf' Tupper, volunteered to be winched down on to a life raft. He unhooked himself, then swam from raft to raft helping the injured and guiding in further waves of rescue helicopters. Chief Petty Officer Tupper was officially credited with assisting in the saving of some fifty lives and was awarded the Distinguished Service Medal.

In a smaller but no less demanding operation a Sea King of No 820 Naval Air Squadron pulled off a technically very difficult rescue on the night of June 1/2 after Flight Lieutenant Ian Mortimer RAF, attached to 801 NAS had to eject from his Sea Harrier about five miles south of Stanley on being hit by a Roland missile.

On reaching his dinghy Ian Mortimer elected only to send a brief voice message over his Search and Rescue Beacon rather than turn on its 'bleeper', possibly leading to him being traced by Argentinian aircraft and captured. In fact a helicopter and a twin-

Lieutenant Commander Hugh Clark's Mark 2 Sea King picking up survivors from *Sir Galahad* *(Reuter)*.

Petty Officer 'Larry' Slater with Lucinda Bell and other survivors.

Chief Petty Officer 'Alf' Tupper *(RNAS Culdrose)*.

engine fixed wing aircraft circled the position where his Harrier had gone in but he had drifted several miles during his parachute descent.

He sent another brief voice message over his 'SARBE' advising any Harriers in the area of a couple of targets but he then saw the Argentinian aircraft turn back to base at last light.

His two brief voice messages had been logged and nine hours after his ejection the 820 Squadron Sea King found him towards the end of a long square search. He switched on his personal strobe light and was plucked to safety by a shipmate from HMS *Invincible*, Leading Naval Aircrewman Mark Finucane.

*   *   *

Early in the morning of 11 August 1985 the stand-by Wessex SAR helicopter at RNAS Culdrose scrambled in response to a

Coastguard request to assist the yacht *Mister Cube* disabled in severe gale conditions about 55 miles south-east of the Lizard. Three adults and six children were reported to be aboard. The yacht's jib had carried away in Force 9 winds and the auxiliary engine had failed to start.

The Wessex, from 771 Naval Air Squadron using callsign 'Rescue 77', lifted off and a Sea King was also brought to readiness at Culdrose. The yacht was found in less than an hour and the Wessex winchman/diver, Petty Officer Laurence Slater, went down.

An initial Hi-line drop was not practical so 'Larry' Slater had to dodge the mast and rigging of the yacht which was rolling through about 40 degrees to get on to the deck first and then supervise the winching. He went up himself with the three youngest children, Lucinda Bell, aged six, and her twin friends Justin and Crispin Sykesball, aged seven. (One problem facing helicopter winchmen during the rescues of small children is that they could fall out of the 'strop' so that this sort of rescue is normally accomplished with the winchmen clutching the children in their arms.)

The adults aboard were safely uplifted too and all recovered quickly after hot baths, a change of clothes and a 'Pusser's breakfast' at Culdrose.

The day was not over, however, for the

The *'Mister Cube'* crew with their rescuers *(RNAS Culdrose)*.

Petty Officer Slater *(RNAS Culdrose)*.

Wessex crew who had landed back at Culdrose at 08:18 hours. They were scrambled again six hours later (having in the meantime given a demonstration at Penzance) following a Coastguard report that another yacht had capsized 1 1/2 miles off Porthscatho. This vessel turned out to be the £1 million, 80-ft long '*Drum England*', owned by the singer Mr Simon Le Bon, leader of the Duran Duran Group.

The Wessex crew, consisting of Lieutenant Coles, (pilot) and Petty Officers Michael Palmer and Larry Slater, found, to their astonishment, the upturned hull of the huge yacht, minus its keel, but with eighteen people sitting and crouching on it and indicating through sign language that there were six more inside the hull.

Larry Slater went down on the wire and then swam to the hull where he obtained from the survivors perched on it an approximate location of the others trapped inside. He dived and entered the upside down hull through a mass of sails and rigging and came to a white hatch cover. Not wanting to waste his precious air supply searching unnecessarily through all the mess he returned to the surface to consult with the others still perched on the upturned hull. They confirmed that the white hatch cover was the correct 'entry point'.

Larry Slater went back down, slid the white hatch cover back and felt his way onwards with hands outstretched. Someone grabbed his hands and he was pulled up into an air pocket to meet six men, including Mr Le Bon, waist deep in icy cold water contaminated with fuel and battery acid, and breathing air laden with diesel fumes.

The Petty Officer introduced himself briefly and explained an escape plan for them all. This, he said, would first necessitate him returning to the aircraft to obtain some breathing equipment for them. 'Don't be long' someone said, according to the official report.

He swam back to the surface, was winched up to the Wessex and returned with the extra breathing equipment. On his next trip down he decided that the breathing apparatus he had brought might, after all, hamper rather than assist the escape because of its bulk and positive buoyancy. Instead he instructed them to take deep breaths and one by one he pulled them out by their ankles.

A written report by a Coastguard officer afterwards stated: 'Remarkably it was all quite orderly — only one survivor got a bit excited, knocking the diver's mask off in the process'.

In just over thirty minutes from the first Scramble order all 24 aboard the *Drum England* were accounted for and the process of shuttling them ashore by helicopter began. Seven months later the Ministry of Defence announced the award of the George Medal to Petty Officer Slater for the work he did on both rescues that day. Lieutenant David Marr and Petty Officer Palmer received Queen's Awards for their part in the *Mister Cube* yacht rescue. Petty Officer Slater, the citation said, 'had shown great fearlessness, superb stamina and unflinching courage in the face of enormous danger'.

The ability of Royal Navy rescue helicopter crewmen not only to descend on a winch wire but to be able to dive as well had never been more clearly demonstrated.

On 24 January 1986 the Greek tanker *Orleans* caught fire 65 miles north-east of Great Yarmouth. The events that followed are best described in the words of the citation for the award of the Air Force Cross to Master Air Loadmaster Melvyn Ward of 'C' Flight, 202 Squadron, at Coltishall. He was the winchman of the Sea King which was scrambled at 07:23 hours.

'In a Force Ten gale with thirty foot waves and burning oil on the sea, the tanker was found blazing fiercely from amidships towards the stern, where the crew was gathered in thick smoke.

'Despite the hazards, Master Air Loadmaster Ward volunteered to be lowered to the deck where, although breathing was difficult, he managed to calm and organise the confused and alarmed foreign crew sufficiently to permit four seamen to be winched up to the helicopter.

'Thickening smoke and a snowstorm then forced the helicopter to stand off. Hearing loud explosions below decks Master Air Loadmaster Ward decided the ship should be abandoned immediately.

'Since the helicopter would be able to recover survivors from the sea, but not from the ship, and with no other means of saving the crew, MALM Ward launched a life raft, briefed the crew to follow him in pairs, and jumped some eighty feet into the water.

'However, none of the crew followed so he swam clear of the stern and was recovered into the helicopter.

'Since conditions now permitted the helicopter to hover over the ship, he again volunteered to return to the deck despite both the danger and his having swallowed a quantity of sea water and oil.

'Although mobbed by the crew he prepared two seamen for lifting but during the lift the winch cable caught and broke on a jackstaff, leaving the two men suspended over the sea. Master Air Loadmaster Ward promptly

The *Orleans* ablaze *(RAF Coltishall)*

Close-up of the conditions Master Air Loadmaster Ward faced on the ship *(RAF Coltishall)*.

recovered them by climbing over the rail and dragging them on board.

'With the helicopter disabled MALM Ward then organised the crew to launch a lifeboat to which improved conditions only now afforded access. Despite breaking all the oars fending off from the tanker this operation succeeded and all occupants were subsequently rescued by a nearby rig support vessel.

'Throughout the operation to evacuate the crew of the *Orleans* MALM Ward displayed in rapidly changing circumstances, exceptional determination, resourcefulness, coolness and courage. His brave and selfless conduct was in the highest traditions of the Royal Air Force'.

The following four incidents exemplify the value of the fixed-wing maritime reconnaissance aircraft as a long-range life-saver even in the helicopter age. Mention has already been made of the contribution made by a Shackleton in the *Lakonia* disaster of 1963.

In February 1960 the 7,000-ton United States freighter *Valley Forge* ran aground on

Master Air Loadmaster Melvyn Ward, AFC *(RAF Coltishall)*.

an island in the South China Sea north-east of Singapore. A Shackleton of 205 Squadron captained by Flight Lieutenant R. Bennett found the ship in fifteen minutes and dropped rescue and survival equipment from 90-ft altitude. (There were at that time no rescue helicopters available at the Shackleton's base of RAF Changi.)

The Second Officer of the ship said later that the equipment nearly fell into their laps. The medical equipment and a dinghy which had been dropped were of particular value because one seaman had been injured and another was suffering from heart trouble. They were both taken ashore in the dinghy. The aircraft then homed in a minesweeper, HMS *Fiskerton,* which took the remainder of the ship's company off twelve hours later.

In March 1964 the North Korean fishing vessel *Chin Glongyin* caught fire in the South Indian ocean with all her lifeboats destroyed. Shackleton *WL786* which was based at Gan, the coral atoll refuelling base roughly in the middle of the Indian Ocean, took off with Flight Lieutenant Peter Bethell as captain and found the ship's crew struggling to make improvised life rafts out of oil drums and spars. They made two passes overhead dropping Lindholme Gear and smoke markers and later homed in the British India liner SS *Nuddea* which completed the rescue.

In September 1977 an adventurous person by the name of Enda O'Coineen set off to cross the Atlantic single-handed in a Zodiac inflatable dinghy. He capsized and initiated a Mayday on his personal locator beacon. He was found in mid-Atlantic by a Nimrod of 120 Squadron from Kinloss, captained by the then Flight Lieutenant Stephen Roncoroni, which dropped Lindholme Gear to him and then homed in the nearby Royal Fleet Auxiliary *Stromness* to complete the rescue.

On 11 February 1982 the 12,000-ton Greek tanker *Victory* broke in half in mid-Atlantic about 450 miles west of the Azores in storm-force winds and 60-ft waves. Fifteen of her crew launched and boarded a lifeboat but it broke up and they were all swept away. Sixteen more crew members stayed aboard the still floating 100-ft long stern section of the ship.

A Belgian freighter, the *Potomac*, closed in and attempted to get a line aboard the stern half of the *Victory*. A Nimrod was scrambled from Kinloss with the First Navigator, Flight Lieutenant John Martin of 201 Squadron as captain (Nimrod captains are not always necessarily the First Pilots).

The first stand-by SAR Nimrod *(XV235)* found the stern half of the ship after a 1,000-mile transit at high 'dash' speed and made radio contact. (The 500-knot approx 'dash'

A Nimrod at St Mawgan with a 236 Operational Conversion Unit crew *(British Aerospace)*.

The stern half of the *Victory* (RAF Kinloss).

speed of the Nimrod in transit to a disaster makes it a most potent world-wide rescuer even if it is thirsty in comparison with the turbo-prop Maritime Reconnaissance aircraft favoured by other nations.)

First of all the crew of *XV235*, using callsign 'Rescue 51' made a low level search for the fifteen who had tried to escape in the lifeboat but found no trace. The Nimrod pilots, Squadron Leader Mackenzie and Flight Lieutenant Cooke, then managed to drop Lindholme Gear across the 'half-ship' in spite of severe turbulence throwing their aircraft about and the violent movement of what was left of the ship.

Shortly afterwards smoke began to emerge from much of Nimrod *XV235*'s high technology search and navigational equipment and the crew had to find their way to the Azores taking sun sights by sextant through the windows, relying on their magnetic compasses and breathing emergency oxygen to combat noxious fumes. Their basic navigational skills replacing the failure of their 'aids' got them home and dry.

Meanwhile another Nimrod, this time from 42 Squadron at St Mawgan in Cornwall, had reached the scene and tried to drop Lindholme Gear in such a way that a line

would link the stern half of *Victory* with the British freighter *Manchester Challenger* which had by then drawn alongside.

A United States Air Force 'Super Jolly Green Giant' from Woodbridge tried to assist in this process and eventually Lynx helicopters from two Dutch frigates winched the last fifteen men to safety.

The *Victory* rescue, though only partly successful, is rated as a classic example of co-operation between nations and between maritime reconnaissance aircraft and surface ships, with the rarely used American 'Super Jolly Green Giants' of the USAF based in Britain playing a significant part.

Several hundred accounts of dramatic rescues from the sea and mountain areas of the United Kingdom have, of course, been written and published in recent years.

The following incidents, described in some detail, must again only be regarded as constituting a cross-section. They have been selected because of somewhat unusual circumstances surrounding each of them.

In January 1981 nine out of twelve members of the crew of a Dutch Atlantique MR aircraft were rescued by a Sea King of 819 Naval Air Squadron from Prestwick after a ditching between the west of Scotland and Northern Ireland. Curiously this was an almost copybook reproduction of a similar operation involving the same rescue unit and the same type of aircraft two years previously in which all fourteen Dutch aircrew aboard an Atlantique were saved.

During the same 48-hour period nine seamen were saved from a sinking Norwegian fishing vessel in that totally inhospitable sea area north-east of Shetland by a combined force of Norwegian Air Force, Bristow and British Airways rescue helicopters. Again RAF Nimrods played a vital part in the search and control phases.

Helicopters often have to rescue the occupants of other helicopters in trouble. In March 1983 a British Airways S-61 'cab' flying from the Piper oilfield to Aberdeen had to ditch 77 miles offshore. A Nimrod in the area made radio contact and homed in an RAF Sea King from Lossiemouth. This helicopter was overhead the 'comfortably' ditched S-61 in one hour and three minutes from the latter's first Mayday call. All

seventeen aboard the S-61 were winched into the Sea King at the rate of two minutes per person. The only difficulty encountered resulted from the puncturing of the S-61's dinghies so that another had to be dropped by the Sea King on a rope.

After the terrible Chinook disaster off Shetland in November 1986 in which 43 oil rig personnel, a pilot and a cabin attendant were lost, there was initially much uninformed speculation about the cause of the crash and criticisms of ditching and safety procedures. It soon became clear, however, that the Chinook disaster was attributable to the greatest fear that all concerned with helicopters have — a 'catastrophic' failure somewhere in the rotor head or gearing mechanism. In the event it was still remarkable that the specially equipped Bristow-owned, Coastguard-contracted S-61 based on rescue stand-by at Sumburgh was actually in the air and was able to pluck out the Chinook's 1st Captain and another survivor before they died of hypothermia even after their lucky escape from the crash impact. The rescue of the 1st Captain, of course, contributed more to the success of the accident investigation than the recovery of any so-called 'black boxes' or pieces of wreckage. The full investigation into the precise causes of this disaster will probably still be going on by the time this book appears.

The 3,600-ton Sealink ferry *Antrim Princess* with 108 passengers on board suffered an engine room fire off the Antrim coast of Northern Ireland in December 1983. Her Master, Captain Thomas Cree, had to order a shut-down of the whole of the ship's electrical system and anchor only half a mile off the rocks of the Island Magee peninsula. Heavy seas swept five life rafts from the decks and it was impossible to launch boats.

All the passengers and twenty crew members were winched to safety in sixty-knot winds by a combined force of Wessex 'Support' helicopters from No 72 Squadron permanently based at RAF Aldergrove during the continuing 'troubles' and by Sea Kings from 819 NAS at Prestwick. The task was completed in just over two hours from the first alarm being given on board the *Antrim Princess* and constituted a good example of how RAF Support helicopter crews can turn

Many photographs of air-sea rescues taken from aircraft, even at quite low altitudes, fail to show the sea conditions being encountered. This 'optical illusion', affecting both the camera lens and the human eye, was the cause of many a flying boat accident in World War 2. This deck-level picture is more revealing. It was taken by Petty Officer Frank de Mengel of HMS *Berwick* during the rescue of a seaman from the German MV *Paaschburg* in the Bay of Biscay in 1979. The survivor is being lowered from the warship's Lynx on to *Berwick's* deck which was pitching about 80 ft at the time. Many rather laconic accounts of helicopter rescues at sea do not bring out the skills and concentrations needed in such almost routine situations *(Frank de Mengel)*.

their hands to a rescue task when the occasion demands.

On 16 November 1984 the 75-ft Inverness registered fishing vessel *Whyalla* radioed that she was taking water and in danger of sinking about ten miles north-east of the BP Forties oilfield off the Scottish coast. Conditions were atrocious with a Force 10 storm creating waves of up to 60 ft but fortunately for the vessel's crew of six help was reasonably close to hand even in this lonely and hostile sea area. It came under the 'self-help' rescue arrangement operated by Bond Helicopters Ltd under contract to BP.

A Bond SA365C Dauphin 2 *(G-BKXD)* based on the oilfield support vessel *Iolair* lifted off in response to the Mayday from the *Whyalla* with Captains David Kinnell and Alan Dent on the flight deck. They fitted a detachable winch and collected winchman John Kelly from the *Forties Bravo* platform.

Meanwhile a Nimrod from Kinloss had located two life rafts. In a typical combined operation the Nimrod (callsign 'Watchdog 02') guided in the civilian rescue helicopter ('Rescue 43').

John Kelly went down on the wire from the Dauphin to look at one of the dinghies but found it empty. The helicopter crew then located the second dinghy and saw it had all of the *Whyalla's* crew aboard. Because of the wave height the helicopter crew first tried to use the Hi-line method but the survivors in the dinghy were too shocked and exhausted to haul the rope in.

John Kelly then went down, unhooked himself, and drew the Hi-line in. He and his friends in the helicopter managed to winch up four survivors in single-lifts in the strop but as the fifth man was about to ascend the dinghy capsized, throwing John Kelly into the sea. Fortunately this fifth man was already secure in the strop and was lifted while John Kelly swam back to the dinghy which the sixth survivor had managed to right.

Another Hi-line had to be dropped because the essential 'weak link' in the first one had parted in the earlier capsize. Eventually both John Kelly and the sixth survivor were winched up into the helicopter. All the survivors were then flown on to the *Forties Alpha* platform where they recovered quickly in spite of severe shock and the swallowing of much sea water.

The ship sank while all this was going on. During the whole operation Captain Kinnell and his co-pilot Alan Dent had had to 'ride the waves', adjusting their own height to the

John Kelly QGM *(Bond Helicopters Ltd).*

rise and fall of the huge waves. This operation was regarded as a classic example of the sort of help which can be given by oil company helicopters to fishing vessels and other craft in distress in this particularly perilous part of the North Sea.

An RAF Sea King from Lossiemouth had been scrambled but would probably have taken too long to reach the scene before the survivors of the *Whyalla* had succumbed to cold.

The skill and courage of the whole crew of the Bond helicopter was recognised by the presentation of the 'Edward and Maisie Lewis Award' from the Shipwrecked Fisherman and Mariners Benevolent Society for the most outstanding air-sea rescue of the year. Many, however, thought that at least John Kelly had deserved some form of personal gallantry award equivalent to those fairly frequently (and justifiably) bestowed upon winchmen and aircrewmen of the RAF and the Royal Navy.

More than two years later, in February 1987, John Kelly received the Queen's Gallantry Medal on the personal recommendation of the Prime Minister, Mrs Thatcher. This was regarded as something of a personal triumph, not only for Mr Kelly but for those who had interceded, and steered their way through Whitehall bureaucracy to see that the crews of civilian rescue helicopters were given equal recognition for their deeds of gallantry.

The Royal Navy and the Royal Marines figured in an unusual rescue in the Antarctic in March 1985. Lieutenant-Commander Clive Waghorn, member of a scientific exploration party, fell and broke a leg 2,500 ft up on a mountain in Brabant Island. He 'holed up' with Lance-Corporal Kerry Gill staying behind to keep him company while others in the party went for help.

After five days there was a break in the extreme weather conditions and a Wasp helicopter from the ice patrol vessel HMS *Endurance* found the two men in a tiny tent. The Wasp pilot, Lieutenant-Commander John White, dropped markers and guided in two Sea Kings from the Royal Fleet Auxiliary *Olna* carrying a doctor and a party of Marines. One Sea King was able to hover at low level on the mountainside and bring

Commander Waghorn and Corporal Gill aboard by ladder. The second Sea King brought back another party of Marines who had managed to reach the scene on foot.

One of those situations about which many in the offshore oil industry have nightmares developed in the first week of November 1985 when the *Tharos* servicing rig in the Forties Field started dragging her anchors in storm to hurricane force winds and was in danger of drifting down on to other nearby rigs.

What is called a 'heads up' message was received at the Northern Rescue Co-ordination Centre in Pitreavie Castle at 21:40 hours on 4 November. Just over an hour later an RAF Sea King from Lossiemouth ('Rescue 37') lifted off with Squadron Leader Martin Cocksedge, the CO of 202 Squadron, acting as First Pilot. He had just happened to be on a visit to his 'D' Flight when the call came through. In the all-officer crew he had with him Flight Lieutenant Brian Murdoch, the 'D' Flight commander, as navigator, Flight Lieutenant Harry Watt as P2 and Flying Officer Rick Bragg as winchman.

A quarter of an hour later the second stand-by Sea King ('Rescue 38') lifted off piloted by Flight Lieutenants Graham Cannell and Doug Scott with Flight Sergeant Bill Reid and Sergeant Paul Barton in the back. At about the same time a Bristow Sikorsky S-61 working under the Coastguard SAR contact was diverted from a task in the Orkneys. It was crewed by Captains Laurence Carmalt and Bob Whitehouse with Chris Bond and Keiran Murphy as winch operator and winchman.

A British Caledonian Bell 214ST, an ordinary oil rig passenger helicopter, was also diverted to the scene piloted by Captain Andrew Beckett with Senior First Officer Ian Maryman beside him.

The aircraft carrier HMS *Illustrious* was also in the area and stood by to launch some of its fleet of anti-submarine Sea Kings. A Nimrod of 120 Squadron, Kinloss, was overhead performing the 'Scene of Search Commander' role.

In the event 140 men were taken off the dragging rig, about fifteen at a time, by the RAF and civilian helicopters. They did not have to resort to winching techniques but hovered over the *Tharos*' helipad low enough

Again the conditions encountered by helicopters in the North Sea oilfields are not always appreciated since it is seldom that anyone has the opportunity to photograph them. This picture was taken by Captain Campbell Bosanquet of British Airways Helicopters showing an S-61 landing on the *Treasure Finder* accommodation rig in a wind strength of 68 knots gusting 78 knots — relatively common conditions. Captain Bosanquet took the picture from his own S-61 while waiting in the queue to land on *(C. C. Bosanquet)*.

for the oil men to walk aboard, but with the pilots still flying them rather than risk blade damage by shutting down in the sixty-knot wind. All were taken to the nearby Forties *Alpha* and *Delta* platforms and eventually the *Tharos* was re-anchored.

Afterwards Squadron Leader Cocksedge said: 'It was a very demanding job calling for all the skills of everyone concerned. What came to me was the efficiency of the organisation. The captain of the Nimrod at 19,000 ft above us was giving clear directions and controlling the helicopter traffic, the BP radio operator on one of the rigs was always cool, calm and collected and giving excellent advice. The people we lifted off were marshalled in groups and seemed to know exactly what they should do.'

The evacuation of the *Tharos* has gone into the annals as a classic task of its kind which went 'according to the book'. It also demonstrated how well Service and civilian helicopters can work together and again demonstrated the important role played by the Nimrods.

A neat 'small one' involving Nigel Mansell, the British Grand Prix racing driver, occurred in June 1986. He was taking helicopter flying lessons at Staveton aerodrome near Cheltenham, when he and his instructor picked up a Mayday call from the pilot of a light fixed-wing aircraft in the vicinity.

Nigel Mansell's instructor, Captain Ted Malet-Warden, took control and they saw a wrecked aircraft on the ground near the runway threshold. They touched down alongside and Nigel Mansell comforted its injured pilot, Mr Philip Robinson, who had suffered an engine failure on his final approach. An ambulance arrived but they put the pilot into their helicopter and flew him direct to hospital where he recovered from relatively minor injuries but considerable shock — which had been alleviated by the helicopter crew's prompt action.

Things did not go well in February 1986 when the trawler *Snekkar Arctic* sank 316 miles west of the Hebrides with a French crew of 27 aboard. Another French trawler in the area picked up nine men from a life raft but the remainder were lost. Some valiant rescue operations were launched including the despatch of Nimrods from Kinloss which searched a 400-square-mile area. A United States Navy Orion maritime reconnaissance aircraft from Iceland also took part in the search.

Rather importantly a USAF 'Super Jolly Green Giant' from Woodbridge accompanied by a C-130 Hercules tanker moved up to Benbecula. If there had been any hope at all for the remainder of the trawler's crew, the 67th Aerospace Rescue and Recovery Squadron, USAF, might have pulled off the first UK rescue involving helicopter in-flight refuelling — something they always hope they may do.

The importance of the informal arrangements with the Republic of Ireland allowing for Royal Navy and Royal Air Force rescue helicopters and Nimrods (strictly speaking 'military aircraft') to overfly Irish air space and refuel on Irish territory was again demonstrated on 23 November 1986 when the Hong Kong-registered 164,000-ton iron ore carrier *Kowloon Bridge* sent out a Mayday announcing that the ship was being abandoned and that helicopter assistance was required.

The ship was wallowing out of control with failed steering gear in busy sea lanes off the south-west coast of Ireland in darkness and in winds gusting up to 75 knots. Fortunately for the Master (Captain T. S. Reo) and his ship's company of 27 this informal 'Anglo-Irish agreement' existed, because the Irish Air Corps at that time and date did not possess rescue helicopters capable of working in total darkness.

The apparently casual requirement by Captain Reo, who later sounded on radio programmes as though he was ringing up for a taxi or two, resulted in two Sea Kings from Brawdy lifting off in the middle of the night. They refuelled at Cork and then uplifted the whole ship's company of the *Kowloon Bridge*.

One of the Brawdy (202 Squadron) Sea King winchmen, Sergeant Barry Hunter, suffered injuries to his hand and shoulder when he was slammed into a hatch cover on being lowered to the ship's deck. Sergeant Hunter said later: 'Basically the ship came up and bit me. But we had to carry on. The two Sea Kings got all the crew off safely in double time. That was what pleased us most. It turned out to be a nice slick job.'

Captain Reo and the owners of the *Kowloon Bridge* faced many questions to answer at the time of writing this chapter. One of them could be why it was *assumed* that rescue helicopters would be available on request without any apparent consideration being given to the safety of *their* crews. Captain Reo did, however, have the grace to praise the work of the 202 Squadron Sea Kings in a radio interview . . .

Chapter Seven
Famine relief

The delivery from the air of food, water and other essentials to human beings in distress can properly be classified as a form of life-saving. The Royal Air Force probably has more experience and has displayed more skill and courage in this form of flying than any equivalent organisation in the world. Its skills were fairly recently demonstrated to the rest of the world during the Ethiopian famine relief operation of 1984/85.

The RAF (or rather as it was then a mixture of the Royal Flying Corps and the Royal Naval Air Service) probably first demonstrated the ability of the aeroplane to succour those in distress on the ground during the siege of a place called Kut El Amara in what was then Mesopotamia, later Iraq in 1916.

A British garrison had been surrounded by Turkish forces and its members were in danger of dying from hunger and thirst. They were part of an Anglo-Indian force which had attempted to march north-west from Basrah to Baghdad during part of the often-forgotten Middle East campaigns of World War 1.

A motley collection of the sort of aeroplanes which had been spared from the Western Front to operate in the Middle East took part in a series of supply drops. They included Short Seaplanes, Voisins and 'Betucis', all rather fragile aircraft. The supplies dropped including flour, sugar, salt, dates, medical stores, parts for a wireless station, mails, a one-mile-long fishing net, 5,000 lira and 80,500 rupees in gold and a mill stone weighing 70 lb which was attached to a parachute.

More than 19,000 lb of food was dropped during 140 flights. Most of the food was carried by the Voisins and Betucis; the Short Seaplanes having some difficulty taking off from water with full loads.

An official report recorded that the food sacks on the Betucis were attached to the lower wings by a cord passing round the butt end of the rear spar. To release them the pilot cut the cords with a knife and tugged the sacks over the trailing edge. Bomb carriers were adapted to supply dropping by removing the bomb guides and fitting a bar, pivoted at one end and fastened by a quick-release attachment operated by the pilot. Loads were carried in two sacks fastened together.

Most of the supply missions were over a 23½ mile distance from Orah. The loads were dropped on to a marked zone to the north of Kut. A contemporary account says that loads were dropped from 5,000 ft altitude, but one suspects that an extra 'nought' might have been added to that record.

The 'double sack' system, later extended to

A fairly early casualty evacuation system adopted by the Royal Air Force. A stretcher case being loaded into a Vickers Vernon in the Middle East *circa* 1920s.

Vickers Vernon *J7541* of 70 Squadron over Baghdad. Note patches on wings. The Vernon was the first aircraft specifically designed for troop carrying duties to enter RAF service — in 1922. It was similar in appearance to the civil version of the Vimy bomber but had a bulbous-shape fuselage with a 'saloon' cabin for up to eleven passengers. Two 450 hp Napier Lions, loaded weight 12,500 lb, maximum speed 118 mph. Wingspan 68 ft 1 in *(Bruce Robertson)*.

a 'treble sack' system, evolved during the air supply to Kut held good for nearly seventy years right up to the Ethiopian 'Operation Bushel'. The whole idea is to pack supplies lightly into an inner sack and then surround it with one or two more, to absorb the impact with the ground.

Between 1921 and 1926 it fell to the Royal Air Force to operate a mail service over the 866 miles of largely desert terrain between Cairo and Baghdad. As a result of World War 1 conquests in the Middle East the British had to establish links between these two capital cities over what had previously been Turkish domain.

Among the RAF squadrons involved in this highly successful operation were two which were to figure again in Ethiopia — Nos 47 and 70 (LXX). The work done by their Vickers Vernons and Victorias, at an early stage supplemented by DH 9as and Vimys from other squadrons, was to lay many foundations for subsequent operations to the benefit of mankind. The whole operation, which often involved casualty evacuations and the 'self-rescue' of downed aircrews, was

brilliantly described by Wing Commander Roderic Hill, MC, AFC, (later Air Chief Marshal Sir Roderic Hill) in his book *The Baghdad Air Mail*.

The Baghdad Air Mail operation was a complete success and although forced landings were relatively frequent and understandable given the 'state of the art' of aviation at the time, no accidents involving serious injury were recorded, let alone fatalities. The 'service' was eventually handed over to Imperial Airways in 1926 as a leg in its 'All Red' commercial airline route to India and beyond.

The navigational system was simple and effective. The aircraft followed a track on the ground made by wheeled vehicles (some of them RAF Rolls-Royce armoured cars) linking a chain of landing grounds. An organisation called the Nairn Transport Company carried heavier loads over part of the route in wheeled and half-tracked vehicles which added their marks to the track on the ground. Sometimes they ran into trouble and had to be assisted by the aeroplanes.

In November 1928 the Shinwari tribe in Eastern Afghanistan rebelled, captured the town of Dakka and took up positions on the

A Vickers Victoria of 70 Squadron over Baghdad. The pilot is Squadron Leader Ryder Young. The Victoria replaced the Vernon in the middle 1920s and most saw service in the Middle East. Two 570 hp Napier Lion XIs. Loaded weight 17,760 lb. Capacity for 22 armed troops. Maximum speed 110 mph at sea level *(Bruce Robertson)*.

A Victoria embarking evacuees at Kabul
(Bruce Robertson).

main road from Kabul to the Khyber Pass, cutting all the road and telegraph communications with India, and taking over the city of Jalalabad. The Afghan Mohmands also moved an army into the Jalalabad area. The British community at Kabul was thereby cut off from the outside world with only an Afghan wireless station and an intermittently working telephone line providing any sort of communication.

On 14 December one Habibullah Khan reached Kabul with an army of a thousand and took ground surrounding all sides of the British Legation. The Head of the Legation, Sir Francis Humphrys, managed to contact the RAF at Peshawar and said he wished to evacuate the women and children of the Legation as soon as possible. He also asked for reconnaissance aircraft to be sent to Kabul.

Twenty-four DH9As and two of the new Westland Wapitis were available in Northern India and there were also ten Vickers Victorias of No 70 (LXX) Squadron plus a Handley Page Hinaidi bomber some 2,800 miles away in Iraq. The latter aeroplanes progressively moved north.

Meanwhile, Flying Officer Trusk set off from Peshawar to Kabul in a DH9A to establish communications and conduct a recce. He first attempted to establish communications by the use of the 'Popham Panel', an early form of air-to-ground communication employing coded symbols which could be laid out on the ground which would be visible to the airman above.

In the course of trying to drop a Popham Panel his aircraft was hit by ground fire which damaged its radiator and fuel pump. He put down quickly and he and his observer managed to reach the Kabul Legation building on foot. He also managed to get off a wireless message and three more DH9As came up from Kabul in succession to continue reconnaissance and maintain communications. All were advised via Popham Panel NOT to land and were assured that all was reasonably well with the members of the British Legation.

By 23 December negotiations between Sir Francis and King Amanulla resulted in permission being given for the evacuation of women and children and a Wapiti, a Victoria of LXX Squadron (piloted by Squadron Leader Maxwell) and three DH9As landed at

Another RAF casualty evacuation task. Assyrian refugees from Mosul arriving at Hinaidi from a Victoria in October 1933
(Bruce Robertson).

Sherpur aerodrome near Kabul. Twenty-three women and children were flown to Peshawar in the Victoria with the DH9As taking the baggage.

On 24 December another 28 women and children, mainly French and German, were evacuated. A German woman was 'unfortunately struck by a propeller', a contemporary account reads. She recovered completely, however, and was evacuated later. The *damaged propeller* was replaced by one from Flying Officer Trusk's earlier downed DH9A, saying much for the improvisations and skills of the airmen of that era, not to mention the abilities of the 'medics' who must have been around.

By early January 1929 the political position had improved and the RAF established a weekly air mail service between Peshawar and Kabul, the aircraft occasionally taking evacuees out on the south-bound legs.

Another internal 'coup' resulted in Squadron Leader Maxwell and Flying Officer Anness flying out ex-King Inayattulla and members of his Royal Family, with their Victorias occasionally under ground fire. Sir Francis Humphrys went on record to say that this task had 'saved Kabul from a horrible massacre'.

Towards the end of January 1929 a final evacuation of the remaining staffs and families of the British and other Legations was, however, considered to be prudent. By this time weather conditions were creating hazards to the aircraft of the age with intense cold and snowstorms often resulting in engine failures in the air and difficulties in starting up on the ground. The task was completed nevertheless, and during the whole operation 586 people of various nationalities were evacuated from Kabul. The RAF flew 28,160 miles in direct evacuation tasks with a grand total of 57,438 clocked up to include the transit flights from Iraq and the odd self-help rescue missions. No lives were lost, and apart from those sustained by the aforementioned unfortunate German lady, no really serious injuries were reported. One Victoria, forced down through engine failure had to be abandoned (and for all anyone knows may still lie somewhere up on 'the North West Frontier') but its crew reached safety on foot after many adventures.

Assyrian refugees in Victoria *K1310* of 70 Squadron en route between Mosul and Hinaidi in October 1933 *(Bruce Robertson)*.

Four officers and five NCOs and airmen were specially commended by the AOC India. He also had much praise in his Despatch for all the ground and air crews concerned for the overall efficiency displayed.

In the remaining 'years of peace' between the two World Wars the Royal Air Force frequently demonstrated the potential of the aeroplane as a saver of life and conveyor of comfort to those in need, not least during the Quetta earthquake of 1935 in which more than 20,000 died and in which the RAF itself suffered grievous losses, including 53 officers and airmen killed.

Almost every RAF aeroplane in India went to help, either to bring in medical supplies, fresh water, food and anything else needed, and also to take out wounded and ill survivors. This often-forgotten episode of the RAF's history is graphically described in Air Chief Marshal Sir David Lee's book *Never Stop the Engine when it's Hot.*

In World War 2 the aeroplane's potential for delivering urgently needed supplies (as well as weapons of war) to otherwise inaccessible places was amply demonstrated and new skills and techniques were developed which would eventually be of benefit to mankind — as so often happens in war. The supply dropping operations at Arnhem, across the Rhine, and perhaps especially in the Far East theatres of war, were all to have a bearing on later, peacetime and humanitarian tasks right up to the recent one in Ethiopia.

These Second World War operations also brought about the creation of an often unrecognised military organisation — the Air Despatch branch first of the Royal Army Service Corps, later of the Royal Corps of Transport. The employment of soldiers at the rear end of transport aircraft was first dictated by a manpower shortage in the RAF but it was quickly recognised as being an entirely logical form of inter-Service co-operation which had come to stay.

The Air Despatch Companies of the RASC, later designated squadrons of the RCT, have earned a proud place in history. More than 100 of them lost their lives in action during World War 2 and after their outstanding deeds at Arnhem they became entitled to wear the 'Golden Dakota' emblems on their sleeves. Four NCOs won Distinguished Flying Medals and numerous awards of MBEs, BEMs and Mentions in Despatches were made plus at least one Military Cross.

The first major peacetime demand upon the RAF to assist civilians in distress after the war came about in early January 1946, when AHQ Burma was told that the Karen tribes in the Lower Shan State were faced with famine because of a rice crop failure. It was assessed that this situation had arisen at least partly because of the help the tribes had given to the Allied cause in fighting the Japanese. Because of this the rice paddies had been neglected and in some areas the Japanese had stopped cultivation.

Accordingly six Dakotas of 62 Squadron and nine Liberators of 355 Squadron were detailed for 'Operation Hunger' with an immediate objective of the air supply of 3,140 tons of rice. The task started on 28 January 1946 and by the end of February 2,326 tons had been dropped. It did not, however end there and more requests were made.

'Operation Hunger' eventually went on into Phases II, III and IV, involving not only the original force of Dakotas and Liberators but also Halifaxes from 298 Squadron and more Dakotas from 10 Squadron. Many lessons were learned which were still applicable nearly twenty years later during 'Operation Bushel' in Ethiopia. They included the development of such procedures as using double, triple or even quintuple sacks (actually first thought of during the Siege of Kut operation). The rice sacks stacked on trays, developed later into the sophisticated pallets used in later operations of the kind.

Perhaps most importantly the 'Hunger' operations demonstrated the hazards of the type of flying involved. The aircraft had to operate in 'hot and high' conditions, often in close proximity to mountain peaks, and drop loads into valleys themselves several thousand feet above sea level. Mists and fogs often descended without warning into the valley floors. Three Dakotas from No 10 Squadron were lost, all on the one day of 29 March during 'Hunger II', and only one crew member survived.

The Berlin Airlift of 1947 and 1948 can of course be classed as a life-saving, or at least a life-support operation but so much has been written about it in the past that it is perhaps only necessary to comment that many more skills and techniques were acquired and perfected during the course of it.

Apart from the military supply dropping operations in such 'minor war' theatres as Korea, Malaya and Borneo, aircraft of the RAF continued to perform many humanitarian tasks in the 1950s and 1960s with their Hastings, Argosies, and Beverleys of what was initially Transport Command, later Air Support Command. One particularly demanding task was the supply of the British North Greenland Expedition in 1952 during which a Hastings was lost but its crew subsequently rescued in a highly skilful operation by a United States aircraft.

The horrific earthquake in Agadir, Morocco, in 1960 drew in help by rescue aircraft from many nations including that done by Shackletons of 224 Squadron based at Gibraltar. Agadir lies about 500 miles south-west of Gibraltar and during the night of 1/2 March ground and air crews loaded supplies into their Shackleton bomb-bay panniers including food, medical equipment and tents.

After off-loading the relief supplies the Shackletons took survivors out to France. Two of them took 42 women and children to Istres with babies being washed in the galleys and their feeding bottles being sterilised in the tea-making machine. Other 224 Squadron Shackletons flew in specialist medical teams

An RAF C-130 Hercules taking part in the 'Khana Cascade' operation in Nepal in the early 1970s. The Lockheed Hercules comes in many versions. The first RAF Hercules made its maiden flight in October 1966. In 1978 a programme began to 'stretch' a number of the RAF aircraft by 15 ft of fuselage length. C-130s of various Marks remain in service all over the Western World with some close copies in service in the East. Basic statistics, four Allison turboprops, maximum loaded weight 155,000 lb-plus, cruising speed about 350 mph. Payload about 46,000 lb *(Lockheed)*.

and on one melancholy occasion 2,400 lb of quicklime urgently needed for communal graves.

By 1970 what was to become the 'Transport Force' of Strike Command had acquired a fleet of C-130 Hercules (quickly nicknamed 'Fat Alberts') aircraft of a type which has brought relief from distress of various sorts to thousands of people all over the world.

During 1971-73 a famine problem emerged in Nepal. An operation labelled 'Khana Cascade' ('Khana' is Gurkhali for 'food') during the course of which nearly 2,000 tons of supplies were delivered either by parachute or by 'heavy free drop' from RAF Hercules aircraft, including a number from 47 Squadron which had now attained a certain immortality in this type of work. The operation, spread over eight weeks, involved a number of parachute drops from about 500 ft altitude and free drops out of the tail doors at altitudes which became progressively lower and lower with 50 ft the norm.

The sorties involved flying among mountains which went up to 26,000 ft with

Everest itself not far away at 29,000. Winds sometimes approached gale force and again the problems of cloud and mist swirling in and filling the valley bottoms had to be coped with. Nevertheless, 187 sorties were flown by fourteen aircraft without accident and at the end of it Mr T. J. O'Brien, the British Ambassador at Khatmandu, reported: 'The Royal Air Force plucked these people from the brink of despair'.

Probably the biggest peacetime famine relief operation in history involving the RAF really began on 26 October 1984 when a planning conference was called at Lyneham, the Wiltshire home of the Transport Force Hercules squadrons.

The first information given out was that a multi-nation relief force was being set up to alleviate extreme famine conditions in Ethiopia, now an 'Eastern bloc country', and that it would entail resources offered by any nation regardless of political allegiances.

The Lyneham Station Commander was also able to tell squadron COs that the operation would have to be entirely self-contained administratively and that it would involve 'air drops' — ie, the throwing-out of food sacks from the Hercules in flight — as well as 'air landings', the much simpler process of merely ferrying cargoes from one usable strip to another.

Numbers 47 and 70 (LXX) Squadrons together with their essential component No 47 (Air Despatch) Squadron, Royal Corps of Transport, began to plan for a major task.

While the Ethiopian government was desperately in need of help from anywhere in the world, suspicions remained about the contributions offered by Western nations. It was revealed more than a year later that many thought that the RAF only went there to spy. Initially the Ethiopian government wanted the RAF to confine itself to air-landing tasks and wanted a two-month commitment rather than the one-month arrangement proffered by HM government.

Meanwhile all concerned at Lyneham got on with their jobs and at one stage demonstrated to the British press and public on Salisbury Plain that they could carry out 'free drops' probably more efficiently than any other air force in the world.

The first messages which came back from a

reconnaissance party of two RAF officers who went to the British Embassy in Addis Ababa suggested that initially at least, air dropping should be ruled out largely because of the lack of facilities both at the aircraft main bases and at up-country dropping zones.

The first RAF Hercules left Lyneham on 1 November 1984 and went to work on straightforward air-landing tasks along with aircraft from many other nations including C-160s of the West German Air Force and AN-12 'CUBs' from a number of Eastern bloc nations. Even at that stage, however, many concerned in the whole operation remained convinced that air-dropping, certainly 'free dropping' rather than parachuting, would be essential if the people really in need were to receive food in time to prevent them actually starving to death.

A free dropping demonstration was carried out 100 miles north of Addis Ababa by an RAF Hercules and a West German C-160 on 23 January 1985 and was entirely successful. It was repeated the following day. Despite some more sucking of teeth among the more politically-minded members of the Ethiopian government and their 'advisers', an

Loading a Hercules during 'Khana Cascade' *(Lockheed)*.

A Hercules with tail doors open carrying out a low-level drop during 'Khana Cascade' *(Lockheed)*.

Back-end scene during 'Operation Bushel' *(RAF)*.

operational free drop of grain was carried out on 26 January at Rabel (9,660 ft above sea level) from an RAF Hercules captained by Flight Lieutenant Jim Norfolk. The free drops then started in earnest from mid-February onwards.

The whole matter of air-dropping is, of course, very much concerned with what the British Services call good 'quarter-mongering'. An often unsung, and sometimes abused breed of officers, Warrant Officers and NCOs exists in the British Army and they are called Quartermasters. One of the best of them was (and still is) Major Alan Batty of 47 (AD) Squadron, RCT. One of his problems in gearing up the Ethiopian relief operation — to become 'Operation Bushel' — was that of keeping costs down to a level which would satisfy his own political masters.

A major cost factor in free dropping operations is that of the pallets upon which sacks of food have to be loaded. Much depends upon whether they be subsequently recovered or not. (This sort of cost factor is multiplied many times in parachuting operations). During UK exercises very expensive pallets made of high-grade thick

Bird strike effect on a Hercules *(RAF Lyneham)*.

plywood are used. Some get bent and broken but can normally be re-used. It was instantly assessed that very few pallets dropped up-country in Ethiopia would ever be recovered.

At current prices a standard plywood 'board' would have cost about £40. Alan Batty, like all good Quartermasters, had his contacts, however, and in a quick trip to Cyprus organised the purchase of equally efficient composition 'boards' at a price of £6 each. He also did some other deals of considerable benefit not only to the starving Ethiopians but also the British taxpayers including one with a remarkable company called Bridport Aviation which resulted in the supply of a vast number of grain sacks at little cost.

'Operation Bushel' eventually went on for more than a year and in total more than 30,000 tons were dropped, most of it by the RAF Hercules crews who rapidly proved themselves to be better at the job than anyone else. At peak periods about 100,000 lb of food a week were being dropped by the RAF aircraft. The same sort of hazards were encountered as during the 'Hunger' and 'Khana Cascade' operations — 'hot and high' flying amongst mountains, mists filling valley floors and cloud shrouding peaks and ridges. There was much turbulence too making the work of the RCT Despatchers and the RAF

Air Quartermasters at the back end particularly demanding. Birds, sometimes enormous ones such as vultures of up to 16 lb in weight, added to the hazards. Someone in the RAF added 'Libyans flying in the wrong direction' to the hazard list . . .

In fact birds nearly brought about a disaster which is perhaps best described in the following citation for the award of a Green Endorsement to Flight Lieutenant R. W. Bond of XLL Squadron. It reads:

'On the 27 April 1985 Flight Lieutenant R. W. Bond, a captain of No 70 Squadron, was flying on "Operation Bushel" famine relief duties in Ethiopia. He was tasked with dropping grain at Rabel Drop Zone, situated in the mountains to the north of Addis Ababa.

'Rabel Drop Zone is 9,000 ft above sea level and the most difficult of the "Bushel" Drop Zones to approach. The profile requires very accurate flying on a curved approach over descending ground below a ridge line. For the drop the aircraft was at 50 ft above ground level; with low airspeed, a high fuel load and extreme payload of 35,000 lb.

'Immediately after dropping an 8,500 lb load with the aircraft pitching down and momentarily out of trim, a flock of birds rose from the ground.

'Eye witnesses on the Drop Zone saw the

bird strike, observed a sheet of flame and when the aircraft pitched down were convinced that it was about to crash.

'A bird had been ingested by No 4 engine which suffered an immediate power loss with visible signs of fire.

'With high ground ahead, and the aircraft in a low speed high drag configuration, Flight Lieutenant Bond was faced with a potentially disastrous situation.

'With exceptional skill he avoided the high ground while simultaneously dealing with the engine failure and fire and reducing the drag.

'It was Flight Lieutenant Bond's first detachment to Ethiopia and he had been in theatre for only two days. The sortie to Rabel was his first operational drop on to this demanding Drop Zone. Flight Lieutenant Bond displayed exceptional flying skill and airmanship in dealing with the emergency at a critical phase of flight.

'In recognition of airmanship and flying skill of the highest order Flight Lieutenant Bond is awarded a Green Endorsement.'

Flight Lieutenant Bond, who later became Flying Instructor at the University of Wales Air Squadron, St Athan, later described the bird strike as 'Not a very nice thing to happen'. He and some friends set up re-enactments of the circumstances and conditions on the simulator at Lyneham and played the whole thing through on five occasions. Five times the simulator computer told him that he and his crew were dead.

The air dropping techniques up-country in Ethiopia called not only for very precise flying to avoid accidents but also to ensure a reasonable success rate in dropping food without undue wastage by burst sacks. The RAF crews began by following the techniques established during 'Khana Cascade' and rolling the pallets out of the tail doors at an altitude of about 50 ft.

A substantial number of food sacks did burst so they began to 'creep' the dropping altitude down — with the benefit of their radar altimeters accurate to within two or three feet of actual ground level — and eventually settled on *ten feet* as the height at which 'the boys in the back room' would actually roll the pallets out.

On the first occasion that a drop was made at this altitude (if one could call it that) a '100 per cent drop' was recorded, meaning that no sacks were seen to burst. On the de-briefing however, the Despatchers and the Air Quartermaster reported something else. This was that the children from the immediate area of the Drop Zone had, as usual, run in to scoop up the spillage from burst sacks and take it home as an immediate aid rather than wait for the official distribution system to take effect. After the '100 per cent drop' these children were seen walking away, very dejectedly, very woebegone.

It is not *officially* recorded but it appears that during subsequent ten-foot altitude drops there were some unfortunate minor accidents with knives and other sharp objects at the back end resulting in a few sacks being split anyway. Humanity can take many forms.

An earlier problem arising from the political difficulties of the Royal Air Force Hercules crews being invited to work with the Russian crews of the MI-8 (HIP) helicopters designated to lay out the Drop Zones in the up-country mountainous areas was resolved rather happily. An organisation called the Polish Relief Helicopter Squadron, also equipped with 'HIPs' arrived on the scene. History went back a decade or two and the RAF and Polish airmen got on very well together.

From that point on there were few if any problems about the essential co-operation between the helicopter crews who had to go up into the mountains first and lay out the Drop Zones and the crews of the RAF's 'Fat Alberts.' This might obviously have had something to do with events going back to the Battle of Britain but whatever the reasons, any remaining ideological barriers were swept aside. One of the treasured possessions at Lyneham is a copy of a long article in a Polish newspaper in which the reporter describes his admiration for the skills and abilities of the Royal Air Force in 1985.

Perhaps another bonus was the presence of Sergeant Boleslaw Zafran of 47 (AD) Squadron, Royal Corps of Transport; Polish born and Polish speaking, and a senior NCO of the British Army. He was diverted from his Air Despatch tasks to become an interpreter, sometimes at very high level. He was awarded the British Empire Medal for his part in the task, which involved him in accepting several 'tours' without home leave.

'Operation Bushel' has been recorded in Royal Air Force records as a satisfying and largely happy task. The flying conditions for the aircrews were extremely demanding and the working conditions for the ground crews equally so. The local allowances paid and the relatively short periods 'on task' plus some quite comfortable living, including billets in an Addis Ababa hotel of note, meant that there was no volunteer manpower shortage.

There were many other spin-offs. Members of both the Royal Air Force and the Royal Corps of Transport in their off-duty hours found many causes to support, such as orphanages, and as usual they all did what they could. Many, like Master Air Loadmaster Bob Jones of LXX (70) Squadron, were so touched with the sights they saw that they went on raising money for causes they thought could help after they returned from the job.

MALM Jones wrote afterwards: 'For many of the relief workers at the camps their first contact with the outside world was the sight of a Hercules descending.

'On the second day of the operation when we landed at—Makele a Land Rover screeched to a halt in front of the aircraft and a young lady leapt out, ran up to me and threw her arms round my neck saying: "It can't be true. Are you really the RAF? Someone does care out there. Thank you." She then burst into tears.'

When they made contact with orphanages and other charitable organisations the RAF personnel found that the greatest need was not always money, but skills and tools to get work done. Since most of them were home-owners and DIY experts in their own right many such problems were solved on the spot. One building urgently needed re-glazing. 'Albert Airways' ferried out some glass bought by LXX crews at Lyneham and it was installed rapidly by the squadron DIY experts. The squadron ground crews rebuilt the workshop at the Leper Colony and a treadle sewing machine was 'acquired' for the girls there to make embroidered tableware for sale to help keep them self-sufficent.

Fund raising specifically for Ethiopian children and for the Save the Children Fund still goes on apace at and around RAF Lyneham. 'Operation Bushel' probably brought the RAF closer to the hearts of people in a remote corner of the world than any of its many life-saving tasks.

A Polish 'HIP' with air and ground crew (RAF).

Chapter Eight
A look at the future

At the time of writing this final chapter at the turn of the years of 1986 and 1987 it did not seem that all that much was urgently needed to improve the airborne rescue facilities available to the citizens of the United Kingdom or to the nation's professional airmen, sailors, and soldiers for whom the 'service' is primarily provided.

On several occasions I have written or proclaimed verbally that Britain has the best air-rescue service in the world and nobody has yet argued with that contention. At this time of writing one 'Gap' had been detected; that of cover over the very hostile sea area to the west and north-west of the Hebrides. There have been one or two occasions when RAF and civilian rescue helicopters have not been able to get to the scene of a disaster in time, in extreme weather conditions, and lives have been lost.

Plans to close this 'Gap' had reached an advanced stage at the end of 1986 with proposals for another contract between the Department of Transport (Coastguard) and a civilian helicopter company to provide a helicopter in the S-61 class at Stornoway. In fact a Bristow S-61 on direct contract to the Coastguard Service began operating in May 1987 from Stornoway and by the end of the year had carried out a number of successful rescues.

More 'civilianisation' was under active consideration at the time of writing. Bristows had submitted a convincing case for taking over virtually the whole of the rescue helicopter Search and Rescue service. Their proposal claimed that this could achieve a 45 per cent saving in the current estimated annual cost of £53 million and that in fact it would be more efficient, particularly from the point of view of civilian rescues which make up about 90 per cent of the total 'trade'.

The Bristow proposal suggested the use of more of specially equipped S-61s, plus Super Pumas and Bell 212s at appropriate locations. These aircraft, they said, would in particular be superior to the RAF and Navy Wessex in night and bad visibility operations.

Understandably there was considerable 'sucking-of-teeth' in RAF and Fleet Air Arm circles. The Navy had by then announced that it would be phasing out its Mark 5 Wessex units at Lee-on-Solent and Culdrose and providing at least one Mark 4 (Commando) Sea King at Portland and modified Mark 5 Sea Kings at Culdrose. In addition the RAF planned to switch the Manston Wessex aircraft with the Coltishall Sea Kings so that the whole of the Channel out into the Western Approaches would have Sea King 'cover'. The Bristol Project was rejected in March, 1968.

By the end of 1987 the Bristow S-61 operation in Shetland was enhanced by the presence of Doctor Chris Rowlands, a local GP with a keen interest in the subject who voluntarily had himself trained in helicopter rescue techniques. Dr. Rowlands, who lives on the edge of Sumburgh airfield assisted in three sea rescues in four days in November 1987. In a way he was following in the footsteps of the redoubtable Dr. David Proctor of Aberdeen who used to fly with the British European Airways rescue helicopters when they operated the direct Coastguard contract in the 1970s. The presence of a doctor aboard is often particularly important in North Sea operations because of the prevalence of accidents involving winch gear among trawlermen.

Another 'Gap' was being examined between the Channel Islands and the French coast, and a plan has been put forward for a commercial operator to provide a rescue helicopter under the Channel Islands defence budget. This proposal remained unresolved at

A Sea King HAR 3 of 202 Squadron. In 1987 the RAF was contemplating making its SAR Squadrons 'All Sea King *(Rolls-Royce)*.

the end of 1987.

Within the Royal Air Force 'search and rescue world', with its operational Wing Headquarters at Finningley and its administrative HQ at Northwood as a part of 18 Group, Strike Command, a great many new ideas were being explored at the turn of 1986/1987. One of these was whether to make the RAF search and rescue squadrons and flights 'all Sea King' instead of five out of the nine of them continuing to operate Wessex Mk 2 helicopters. Much argument about this was to go on into 1987 and beyond. The air and ground crews of the RAF Wessex SAR flights at Leuchars, Leconfield, Manston, Chivenor and Valley remained convinced that their aeroplane type, irrespective of its 32-year-old design age, was the ideal one for quick scrambles and especially for mountain work.

The problem for the long-term planners, however, was whether other branches of the RAF and the Navy would have to drop the Wessex out of their equipment lists and whether there would be sufficient technical back-up in terms of spares and maintenance facilities. By 1987 the Fleet Air Arm was beginning to look to the EH 101 as a replacement for its anti-submarine warfare Sea Kings, but was equally looking forward to more Mark 4 'Commando' Sea Kings to replace the last of its troop-carrying Wessex. The whole of the helicopter world is therefore fluid at the time of the publication of this book.

Several more immediate matters were,

however, also under consideration. In the early years of the employment of the HAR 3 Sea Kings in the RAF search and rescue flights problems were encountered with the hydraulic winches and a school of thought pointed out that it would be incredibly wasteful for one of those expensive aircraft, with an expensively trained crew, to flog its way through gales or storms for 200 miles, reach the scene of a disaster, only to find that the winch wouldn't work.

Ideas for a second winch on the Sea Kings were therefore put forward at a fairly early stage and the death of Master Air Loadmaster Bullock, referred to earlier, did have a 'catalyst effect' on this line of thinking. Even in these days of high technology, however, it has NOT been a case of no sooner thought of than done. One system, providing for an electrically-powered winch mounted aft of the existing hydraulic one, has proved unsatisfactory because of centre-of-gravity problems. Experiments are now going on into the provision of a detachable electric winch, normally stowed in the aircraft, which could be fitted in an emergency; not unlike those used by the British Airways S-61s earmarked for occasional rescue tasks.

(All rescue helicopters do have a final 'fall-back' system in the form of the 'Heave-ho' hoist, which is really only a refined form of any sailor's block-and-tackle gear, which can be used at low altitudes, given quite a lot of time and a great deal of muscular power on the part of the winch operator.)

Experimental work was continuing into the provision of direct voice communication between the winchman on the end of the wire — perhaps 250 ft below his aeroplane — and his winch operator to at least supplement the well proven hand signal and mental telepathy arrangement which has stood the test of so much time.

Even in the era of high technology in the communications field this was still proving a difficult problem to surmount. In the Dragonflies of the 1950s a telephone cable was spliced into the winch wire but it seldom, if ever, worked properly because immersion into salt water almost always produced a set of ear-bending crackles. This form of communication failure presented particular problems for the Dragonfly crews since they

This 1950s picture of a Dragonfly shows an early attempt to provide voice communication between winchman and pilot. The 'phone wire' is wrapped loosely round the winch cable. In the event it nearly always shorted out in contact with sea water. The problem had still not been completely solved by 1987 *(Royal Navy)*

were 'two-man jobs' and the pilot had to raise or lower his crewman on the winch via a button on his cyclic-pitch column, with no view at all of what was happening to his mate underneath. The problem was partly solved by fitting highly polished hub caps from Humber staff cars to the undercarriage legs as convex mirrors. That form of expediency, like so many improvisations, DID work.

The current research is directed towards the

Modern rescue facilities in the North Sea oilfields have been enhanced by the provision of a fleet of Dauphins operated by Bond Helicopters *(Bond)*.

provision of a mini-radio inside the winchman's bone-dome helmet but in the year of 1987 the best brains in the telecom business had still not got it quite right.

The matter of 'compatible' radio communications between both rotary and fixed-wing rescue aircraft and other agencies on the ground had reached an advanced stage by 1988, although there was still a tiny problem involving the reluctance of certain Chief Constables to allow anyone except policemen to use their radio nets.

In the early days of helicopter rescue operations there were some ludicrous gaps in this essential form of communication with the aircraft sometimes only having UHF sets over which they could talk to other aeroplanes and RAF ground stations but no one else. 'Compatibility' has, however, been successively improved down the years with a helicopter or Nimrod crew being able to talk to anyone else involved in the rescue task, including perhaps the owner of a 20-ft yacht who has a little VHF set aboard or someone stuck on a mountain with a pocket 'walkie-talkie'.

An important advance was being made at

the turn of 1986-87 in the field of first-aid training and medical qualifications held by RAF helicopter winchmen. The medical profession within the RAF had for some time disapproved of winchmen being offically allowed to do much more than St John Ambulance Certificate holders when treating casualties. Winchmen are now, though, being trained and qualified to use some of the more advanced forms of resuscitation equipment and use certain pain-relieving techniques. As in many other fields the strict rules have occasionally been 'bent' in life-or-death situations. The story is told, but perhaps for good reasons never formally confirmed, of a Royal Air Force Sergeant carrying out what amounted to a surgical operation with his winchman's knife and the tube from a ballpoint pen on the side of a mountain.

His survivor survived. Had he not the NCO concerned might have had a lot of difficult questions to answer at an inquest. There is no doubt at all, however, that the survivor would have died if the Sergeant had not done what he did. Both lived and prospered in later years, including the Sergeant whose subsequent successful career in the Royal Air

Force owed much to this and several other deeds, which did not always conform to 'the book'.

In 1986 the Royal Air Force Marine Branch was 'civilianised'. Its proud history is being written by another author. From the mid-1950s when the helicopter became the prime rescuer of downed aircrews at sea the Branch's rescue role diminished although it continued to play a major part in the training of both helicopter rescue aircrew and aircrew in general. Under the 'civilianisation' programme the same boats continued to operate from places like Holyhead and Mount Batten on rescue training exercises, the only noticeable difference being that their crews wore dark blue Merchant Navy uniforms instead of light blue RAF ones and that Sergeants seemed to have become 'Second Officers' and the like. Most of them were the same people.

The last of the RAF launches to have a prime rescue responsibility were based at Gibraltar where there were no SAR helicopters available and where helicopters never like flying very much anyway because of the downdraughting and turbulence problems off 'The Rock'. This responsibility was taken over by the Navy while the rest of the Marine Branch boats were taken over by James Fisher Limited.

The RAF's helicopter rescue facilities outside the UK remained important and to some extent expanded during the 1986/87 period. Ever since the conclusion of the Falklands War of 1982 a detachment of No 202 Squadron's Sea Kings has been in position there with air and ground crews being rotated from the UK based Flights.

In Cyprus, what was a United Nations rescue helicopter unit equipped with Mark 2 Wessex has been transferred back to full RAF control as a component of No 84 Squadron with its aeroplanes now painted yellow, like those of the UK flights.

In many of the other corners of the world where the British armed forces still operate helicopters are available for rescue tasks when needed, say in Hong Kong or Belize. The Army Air Corps also continues to play a humanitarian role in the use of its Hong Kong-based aircraft.

During the 'deep freeze' of January 1987

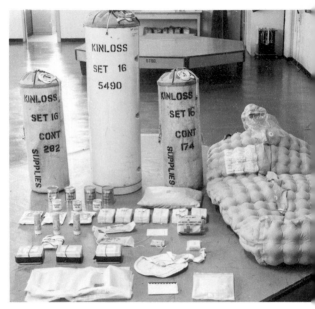

Lindholme Gear and an emergency single-seat life raft as carried at all times by RAF Maritime Reconnaissance Nimrods. The basic principles of the Gear, shown alongside some of the 'goodies' dropped to survivors, have remained unaltered since it was invented by Air Commodore Waring in the early years of World War 2 *(RAF Kinloss)*.

rescue helicopters were busy throughout the British Isles. Several members of the next generation owe their entry into life to them as their mothers were conveyed to maternity hospitals from remote and cut-off locations. Many winchmen and aircrewmen took 'crash courses' on midwifery during this period and some were rather sorry they never actually practised the art, though there were some 'close-gos'.

The 'air rescue component' of the ferry disaster at Zeebrugge on 6 March 1987 tended to be somewhat underwritten at the time in the welter of information which had to be obtained and disseminated.

A look back shortly afterwards (just in time for inclusion in this book) showed very clearly however that without the excellence of the air rescue organisations in Britain and on the other side of the Channel many more than 135 people might have perished and fewer than 400 rescued.

The exact timing of the final capsize of the

7,951-tonne *Herald of Free Enterprise* remains in some doubt but certainly the Acting Master of a dredger, the *San Deros* saw her lights tilt and then go out at 19:46 ('quarter to eight') Local Time. This was equivalent to 18:46 or 'quarter to seven' Greenwich Mean Time.

The dredger's Acting Master, Robert Heinemann, instantly transmitted a 'Mayday Relay' message meaning that he was reporting another ship in acute distress. From that moment a sharply honed West European/NATO rescue system went into action.

The first reaction came from the Belgian Air Force base at Koksidje, only about 30 miles from Zeebrugge. Within 15 minutes of Robert Heinemann's RT call two rescue Sea Kings were hovering over the side of the ferry's hull and starting to winch up a total of 28 survivors who included eight-year-old Martin Hartley who lost his parents, grandparents and an 'unofficial aunt'; and a young women in her ninth month of pregnancy who survived and later gave birth naturally to her child.

(The Belgian Air Force Westland-built Sea Kings, officially classified as 'Mark 48s' but virtually equivalent to the RAF's HAR 3s

'Safe Delivery'. A 202 Squadron Sea King from Boulmer disembarks a lady from Berwick-on-Tweed at Newcastle-upon-Tyne during the January 1987 freeze-up. She later gave birth to a 7lb 12 oz girl. Two other injured people were aboard and the flight had been a difficult one involving several precautionary landings during nil-visibility snowstorms. A number of helicopter crewmen took crash courses in midwifery in January 1987 and while no children were actually born in the air there were some 'close-calls' *(Doug Hall, Stewart Bonney News Agency, Newcastle-upon-Tyne)*.

were purchased in 1974 with their first crews trained at RNAS Culdrose. The Belgian Sea King crews train frequently alongside the RAF and the Fleet Air Arm and have 'total compatibility' — a factor which may have aided the rescue operations considerably on the night of 6/7 March 1987.)

By 19:10 hours GMT ('ten past seven') the British Southern Rescue Co-ordination Centre at Mount Wyse, Plymouth received an alert and its Duty Contoller, Flight Lieutenant Wilkins, pressed all the buttons at his disposal. This officer had considerable 'clout' because contingency plans for maritime disasters were in his and others' minds, if not actually on paper.

Flight Lieutenant Wilkins's action resulted among other things in the rapid scramblings and lift-offs of seven British Sea King helicopters.

First off the ground was 'Rescue 196', a Sea King of No 706 Naval Air Squadron on rescue stand-by at RNAS Culdrose in Cornwall. It was followed by an RAF Sea King ('Rescue 125') from Coltishall in Norfolk, then by 'Rescue 190' from Brawdy, Pembrokeshire; 'Rescue 131' from Boulmer, Northumberland; 'Rescue 197' (another RN aircraft from Culdrose); 'Rescue 132' from Boulmer, and 'Rescue 199' from the RAF Sea King Training Unit at Culdrose.

Flight Lieutenant Wilkins and others at Mount Wyse then had to decide how to deploy their Sea Kings to the best effect. It soon became clear that their most important task would be to lift expert divers and heavy equipment as quickly as possible to the Zeebrugge area — the initial lifting of survivors already being carried out by the Belgian Sea Kings supported by surface vessels.

The British helicopters were therefore routed through the night to such pick-up points as Roborough (Plymouth); Lee-on-Solent and Portland to collect the best divers in the world and fly them on. Manston was selected as the final concentration point — the old Kentish airfield which had borne so much brunt in the Battle of Britain, still a major Rescue base, and capable of handling anything thrown at it. Not only did the Sea Kings arrive, refuel and re-load at Manston but a Hercules from Lyneham lobbed in,

threw out its SAS parachutists which it had been carrying on an exercise and re-loaded with Kent firemen and their equipment and took off again.

A Navy Jetstream communications aircraft went in and out loading up specialists and special equipment and a Nimrod from Kinloss, called out in case there was need for it to act as 'Scene of Search Commander' (see references to the *Alexander Kielland* disaster) lobbed in and acted as a load carrier.

A Sea King of 820 Squadron from HMS *Ark Royal* transfers a survivor from the *Hessen* to another fishing vessel with John O' Groats in the background. The last off were the *Hessen's* Master, Captain Ottmar Krohn and Warrant Officer Anthony Benton, in charge of the salvage team put aboard from *Ark Royal*.
An officer of the carrier said: 'The sight of the ship sinking was a sad and poignant reminder to all of the dangers of life at sea, the more so since it was set against a background of unspoilt Scottish countryside'.
(Royal Navy)

Sea Kings from 820 Squadron, HMS *Ark Royal* were overhead the sinking *Hessen* within minutes of Wick Radio rebroadcasting the vessel's Mayday signal. *(Royal Navy)*

The morning after Manston became the departure point for VIPs such as the Duke and Duchess of York and Mrs Thatcher wanting to get to Zeebrugge as quickly as possible to offer such comfort as they could.

The seven British Sea Kings deployed flew a total of more than 80 hours. Although unable to carry out any direct rescues of survivors, several of them lifted exhausted divers off the hull of the ship and dropped fresh teams in. All of those concerned to whom this author was able to speak said they wished they could have done more, and many said that if the disaster had happened 20 minutes later, ten miles further out to sea, perhaps only they *could* have helped.

Perhaps the only happy outcome of the Zeebrugge disaster was that 400 lives *were* saved; many of them by the excellence of the rescue services in and around the United Kingdom's shores.

The international nature of many air sea rescues was well illustrated in March 1987 when United States Coastguard Helicopters lifted 37 people, including a women and a baby, from a sinking Russian freighter off the New Jersey coast.

The Royal Navy's ability to assist in civilian rescue work from warships at sea was well demonstrated on two occasions in the summer of 1987.

On June 26 HMS *Ark Royal* was near at hand when the 998-ton West German trawler *Hessen* began to sink in the Pentland Firth off John O'Groats.

Ark Royal's Sea Kings first winched down a salvage team with pumps and later assisted to rescue all 19 crew members plus some of their own shipmates before the vessel finally foundered.

On July 3 Richard Branson's spectacular crossing of the Atlantic in his huge balloon 'Virgin Atlantic Flyer' nearly ended in disaster when he and his co-pilot Per Lindstrand had to jump from it, one after the other, into the Irish Sea.

The frigate HMS *Argonaut*, with its own Lynx helicopter aboard, and Sea Kings from 819 Naval Air Squadron at HMS *Gannet,* Prestwick, were however around to help.

When Scottish Military Air Traffic Control reported that the balloon had touched the water and bounced off about 28 miles north of Portrush the search-and-rescue stand-by Sea King at Prestwick was scrambled.

Another 819 Squadron Sea King on an anti-submarine exercise diverted to the area.

Richard Branson himself, who had jumped just after the balloon's second bounce was quickly picked up by HMS *Argonaut's* Lynx. Per Lindstrand, who had jumped earlier from an altitude of 70-feet was picked up by a

'Rescue 177', HMS *Argonaut* and 'Virgin Atlantic Flyer' on the evening of July 3. *(Royal Navy).*

privately owned high-speed inflatable launch which was guided to him by the 819 Sea King using Callsign 'Rescue 177'.

Within minutes the Sea King had lifted Richard Branson from *Argonaut*'s deck and Per Lindstrand from a beach at Portrush; re-uniting them and thereby quelling Richard Branson's main concern that his co-pilot might have lost his life.

'Rescue 177' then took both men to Crosshouse Hospital, Kilmarnock, with Medical Assistant Mark Stephenson and Leading Aircrewman Robert Yeomans giving them some in-flight treatment for exposure and shock.

The whole rescue operation, from the 819 Squadron scramble to the two men arriving at the hospital took one hour 35 minutes.

The rest of the aircrew of 'Rescue 177' were Lieutenants Martin Rayner, Chris Highton and Martin Tilley and Leading Aircrewman (Phot) Philip Ball who took the accompanying historic pictures.

The last words of this book therefore cannot contain anything much in the way of criticism, only a repetition of the praise which the author feels all concerned so richly deserve.

Per Lindstrand and Richard Branson re-united in 819 NAS Sea King 'Rescue 177'
(Leading Aircrewman [Phot] *Philip Ball).*

Index